"*The Changemaker* is a must read for anyone who wants to make a positive impact on the status quo. Deke's practical and pragmatic advice offers a heartfelt and authentic view into what is required of successful leaders ... or at least should be required. Deke embodies one of my favorite lines from my favorite band, U2: 'She's packing a suitcase for a place none of us has seen, a place that has to be believed to be seen.'"

**—Monty Hamilton**

*CEO, Rural Sourcing Incorporated*

"Deke is a complete public servant, which is all too rare these days. He is a true independent who is not saddled with party ideology and group think. He has demonstrated that a dedicated leader can bring positive change and inspire their team to reject political expediency in working for the common good of the citizenry. My wife and I met Deke, Malisa, and their delightful family at their wedding in Bermuda twenty years ago. As a director of the Bermuda Community Foundation, I organized a gathering of the Bermuda government and business leaders who enjoyed the benefit of Deke's experience. I highly recommend Deke as a resource for leadership in addressing challenges facing business and public organizations."

**—Brian O'Hara**

*Former President and CEO, XL Capital*

"As a community leader, Deke Copenhaver's inspiring memoir is a primer for anyone looking to shake up the status quo and become a Changemaker."

**—Jay Samit**

*Bestselling Author,* Disrupt You!

"Ninety percent of people are ready for change, but only ten percent are ready to change. *The Changemaker* is the best book for those who are ready to change and gives readers the resources to make it happen. Read it to change your life so you can change the lives of people around you."

**—Mark Goulston**

*Author,* Just Listen: Discover the Secret to Getting Through to Absolutely Anyone

"To know Deke is to know a great human being. The love and respect that he and dad shared was special. I witnessed it at the Tour de Georgia and many other times. His service to mankind and his community is a platform for change. Thank you, Deke!"

**—Deanna Brown Thomas**

*President, The James Brown Family Foundation*

"With the trials and tribulations around us today, it's time to tap into your inner Changemaker and make a real difference in your world. Deke's passion comes through in equal part substance and story. It is entertaining and educational, and most of all inspiring. *The Changemaker* shows from the start that everyone can lead their world to a better place. If you want to improve your status quo, don't wait for others. Read this book and learn—chapter by chapter—each step in a process that can make you the leader that people will be proud to follow."

**—Tom Patterson**

*Author,* Mapping Security

*Security Advisor, DoD, FBI, NASA, and the White House.*


"Smart people will love this book. It challenges us to lead and implement positive, lasting change through listening and consensus rather than bullying and grandstanding. Deke gives us tools to connect and be open to growth outside of our comfortable zone. And most importantly, he lets us learn from his successes and failures. This book is a unifying call to the right kind of action, just when we need it most."

**—Eric Zachrison**

*Founder, Context*

# THE CHANGEMAKER

# DEKE COPENHAVER

*the*

# CHANGE
# MAKER

the art of building
better leaders

**Forbes**Books

Published by ForbesBooks, Charleston, South Carolina.
Member of Advantage Media Group.

ForbesBooks is a registered trademark, and the ForbesBooks colophon is a trademark of Forbes Media, LLC.

Printed in the United States of America.

10  9  8  7  6  5  4  3  2  1

ISBN: 978-1-946633-73-6
LCCN: 2019937850

This publication is designed to provide accurate and authoritative information in regard to the subject matter covered. It is sold with the understanding that the publisher is not engaged in rendering legal, accounting, or other professional services. If legal advice or other expert assistance is required, the services of a competent professional person should be sought.

Advantage Media Group is proud to be a part of the Tree Neutral® program. Tree Neutral offsets the number of trees consumed in the production and printing of this book by taking proactive steps such as planting trees in direct proportion to the number of trees used to print books. To learn more about Tree Neutral, please visit **www.treeneutral.com**.

Since 1917, the Forbes mission has remained constant. Global Champions of Entrepreneurial Capitalism. ForbesBooks exists to further that aim by bringing the Stories, Passion, and Knowledge of top thought leaders to the forefront. ForbesBooks brings you The Best in Business. To be considered for publication, please visit **www.forbesbooks.com**.

*For my wife, Malisa, without whose love and support this book never would have been possible. And for all of our family and friends from all walks of life who have always been there for us every step of the way.*

# table of contents

## Becoming a Changemaker

## The Outsider

## What Kind of a Leader Are You?

# foreword

As a reformed philosophy major turned new urbanist developer (preservationist, soldier in the war against childhood cancer, involved citizen, parent, father ...), I often reflect on my life's landmark decisions with an instinctive degree of consideration as to their nature and substance. One common thread throughout these major life moments is that all, by their nature, represent responses to change, be they conscious responses to my circumstances or reactions to outside changes beyond my control. Each represents a single footprint, marking how I got here, and serve as touchstones where I can ask: "Were these decisions made sincerely ... selfishly ... faithfully ... for myself or others?"

Many of these benchmarks affected true, life-altering change, such as my middle son's diagnosis with, what we were told to be, a hopeless subtype of pediatric leukemia and the imperative nature of either pressing on or accepting the worst. Some represent moments where self-reflection on my place in time as a professional, citizen, husband, and father inspired watershed impulses of determination to take a risk for, hopefully, the right reason. I would love to have a second chance at many, but the most meaningful are when I decided I needed to attempt positive change or risk regret.

Having said all this, I can confidently say that until my mid-thirties, I found myself back in my hometown trying to find my place and drawn to the authentic sincerity of Deke Copenhaver. Both of us had recently left careers in dynamic southeastern cities to make a new start in a place that we loved, but also in a community that had been lagging in many ways. We became mutual sounding boards for each other, philosophizing on how we could help create a better community and kindle a greater sense of civic pride in others. To this extent, I had never considered myself as a "Changemaker." But now, reflecting on life's twists and turns, I could not have rendered myself capable without Deke's willingness to take the lead and set the standard.

This extremely well written and insightful book could not be more aptly titled, as Deke truly is a Changemaker. While our modern culture deifies those who gamble financial risk, Deke is a guy who is willing to take on the more precarious risk of reputation, demonstrating that real value is galvanized through honesty, empathy, and a willingness to break conventional barriers. This is how we, and therefore our communities, grow and prosper.

Today we live in a treacherous social and political climate where—for reasons of party, pride, or outdated principle—the refusal to change and listen to others clouds the path forward. But Deke is an exception. He is a pathfinder, one who endures the thorns and brambles and opens a way forward. I know, because his footprints have made my path easier; and I am both grateful and excited that he has documented a roadmap in *The Changemaker*.

**—N. Turner Simkins**

Turner Simkins is the author of *Possibilities*, a bestselling memoir about his family's experience with, and personal change through, childhood cancer. A graduate of Washington and Lee University, he is an entrepreneurial real estate developer and lives in Augusta, Georgia with his wife and three sons.

# acknowledgments

There are so many people in my life who have supported me through the years and contributed to this story that it's hard to know where to begin. To my beautiful bride, Malisa, thank you for always believing in me and supporting me in all of my professional endeavors. I'd like to thank my parents, Jane and Bill, for bringing me into this world and for raising me with loving kindness. To my brothers, Andy—whose presence in our lives is sorely missed—and John, thank you for a lifetime spent together and for your influence in my life. Thank you to my sisters, Paula and Lisa, for being there for me throughout my life and for being great examples of what strong women mean to the world.

To all of our nieces and nephews, many thanks for being the younger brothers and sisters I never had, and for giving life to a new generation of our family. To my grandparents, all of my aunts and uncles, and a multitude of cousins, thank you for being a family I'm proud to be a part of. Many thanks to our colorful cast of friends who provide us with joy and comfort on a daily basis, and to our very special friend, Gaines Hitson, for being there for Malisa and me every day.

Thank you to my mother- and father-in-law, Kitty and Bruz, whose love and unwavering support we sorely miss. Thank you for raising an amazing woman in your daughter. Many thanks to all of our in-laws for providing a lifetime of wonderful family memories through our times together. Thank you to all of my mentors and spiritual advisors through the years who have shared with me wisdom and life experiences which have contributed to who I am and have challenged me to be a better man.

To Mayor Joe Riley of Charleston, thank you for being my role model during my time in office. Thank you to Congressman Doug Barnard for your unwavering support of me during my first run for office, and please know that your statesmanlike leadership is missed in our community and throughout this nation.

Thank you to the citizens of Augusta for your overwhelming support during my time in office and in all of my endeavors since. To all of the people I had the pleasure of working with through three campaigns and nine years in office—including our internal leadership team of Fred Russell, Karyn Nixon, Natasha McFarley, and Al Dallas—many thanks for making my job so much easier and for your commitment to making Augusta a better place for all of its citizens. Thank you to Virginia Claussen and Bethany Davis for helping to create a one-of-a-kind radio show and for all of the fun we had in the process. To Malisa's entire family, thank you for all of your support and encouragement for us during our two decades together.

Many thanks to all of my clients past, present, and future for allowing me the opportunity to help strengthen and grow your businesses, your nonprofits, and your communities in creative and oftentimes unconventional ways.

To the next generation of leaders here in Augusta, many thanks for the opportunity to mentor you and to be inspired by you each and every day. To my Advantage|ForbesBooks team, thank you for being so fun to work with and for making authoring this book a wonderful experience as well as for providing me a platform to deliver a message of hope.

A very special thank you to Brian O'Hara, Jay Samit, Tom Patterson, Mark Goulston, Monty Hamilton, Deanna Brown Thomas, and Eric Zachrison for taking time out of your busy schedules to contribute testimonials to the book. And a heartfelt thank you to my inspiring friend, N. Turner Simkins, for contributing a foreword that nearly brought tears to my eyes.

Finally, thank you to the Good Lord for blessing me with an amazing life and for never letting me go, despite every twist and turn.

## about the author

Deke Copenhaver currently serves as principal of Copenhaver Consulting, LLC, a niche consulting firm in Augusta, Georgia, serving the needs of businesses, nonprofits, and local governments. Deke served as mayor of Augusta, Georgia from 2005 through 2014. Since leaving office, Deke has served as the host of *There it is ... With Deke Copenhaver*, a daily call-in radio show on WGAC New Talk Radio, as well as managing consultant for the Augusta Economic Development Authority.

Deke has spoken at many national conferences on topics including city design, economic development, healthcare, veterans' issues, and the nonprofit industry. He currently authors a monthly column on leadership published by the Georgia Municipal Association. Deke earned a BA in political science from Augusta College and is a graduate of Leadership Georgia and the Mayors' Institute on City Design.

Deke has been recognized as one of *Georgia Trend's* "100 Most Influential Georgians" seven times. In 2012, *Southern Living* named Deke as one of their "Heroes of the New South" for his passionate work in helping to revitalize Augusta's historic inner-city African American neighborhoods. In 2010, he was awarded the "Exemplary Service for Community Unity" award by the Martin Luther King, Jr. Memorial Committee. Deke was the 2013 recipient of the Robert F. Cocklin Award presented by the Third Region of the Association of the United States Army for his exceptional support of AUSA, our nation's military and their families. In 2014, the Greater Augusta Arts Council recognized Deke with the President's Award for his support of and commitment to the arts. In 2017, he was recognized by Leadership Augusta with their Ruth Crawford Community Leadership Award. In 2017, Deke was presented with the First Annual Invest Augusta Cyber Leadership Award.

During his final reelection campaign in 2010, Deke became the first American mayor to complete all three legs of a sanctioned IRONMAN event and has subsequently completed four more IRONMAN 70.3s. He and his lovely wife, Malisa, reside in Augusta, Georgia with their three dogs: Sarah Bet, Buddy, and Johnny.

# t i m e l i n e

1997—Became a partner in the real estate firm Huffines, Dukes and Copenhaver LLC.

1999—Moved home to Augusta and married his wife, Malisa.

2001—Hired as executive director of the Central Savannah River Land Trust.

2003—Recognized by *Georgia Trend* as one of the "Forty under Forty" young professionals.

2004—Appointed by Governor Sonny Perdue to serve on the Georgia Land Conservation Partnership Advisory Council; graduated from Leadership Georgia.

2005—Elected mayor of Augusta, Georgia to fulfill an unexpired term; the passing of Malisa's mother, Kitty Boardman.

2006—Reelected mayor of Augusta for his first full term; announcement of Automatic Data Processing bringing a thousand jobs to Augusta; James Brown passes.

2007—First recognition by *Georgia Trend* as one of the "100 Most Influential Georgians."

**2008**—Initial funding approved for the Laney-Walker Bethlehem Revitalization Initiative; recognized with the Distinguished Alumni Award by Augusta University.

**2009**—Named a Paul Harris Fellow by the Rotary Foundation of Rotary International; American Recovery and Reinvestment Act begins its implementation in Augusta; Deke's father, Bill Copenhaver, passes.

**2010**—Reelected mayor of Augusta; Augusta hosts its first Pride Parade; Deke completed his first IRONMAN 70.3; met Tiger Woods.

**2011**—Targeted by the Georgia Gun Owners Association and the Freedom From Religion Foundation; initiated into the National Honor Society of Phi Kappa Phi; graduated from the Mayor's Institute on City Design; received the Exemplary Service for Community Unity Award from the Martin Luther King Jr. Memorial Committee.

**2012**—Named by *Southern Living* as a "Hero of the New South" for being a part of the Laney-Walker Bethlehem Revitalization Initiative; Starbucks announces new $172-million-dollar manufacturing facility in Augusta, creating 140 new jobs.

**2013**—Received the Robert F. Cocklin Award from the Association of the United States Army for outstanding support for AUSA, our nation's military and their families.

**2014**—Final year in office; Unisys announcement of seven hundred new jobs for Augusta.

**2015**—Started Copenhaver Consulting LLC; Malisa's father, Bruz Boardman, passes; first TEDx talk, *Cities: Where All Things Connect.*

**2016**—Began hosting *There it is ... With Deke Copenhaver.*

**2017**—Named managing consultant of the Augusta Economic Development Authority; Starbucks breaks ground on $120 million expansion, creating one hundred new jobs; Deke's brother, Andy, passes from pancreatic cancer.

**2018**—Named "Best Politician" by the readers of the *Metro Spirit.*

# Becoming a Changemaker

*True power, in any leader, is the power to inspire.*
**—DEKE COPENHAVER**

I never grew up dreaming of running for office. Ironically, I grew up dreaming of being a writer. In the end, however, I lived my life by going where I saw the most need. And in 2004, in my hometown of Augusta, Georgia, the need was great.

I was just shy of thirty-seven years old and had been through a myriad of life-changing moments at a relatively young age, having lost my first wife to suicide and then my mother to cancer prior to the age of thirty, while at the same time having had success in my business and nonprofit ventures. Life was, is, and always will be a mixed bag for any of us focused on changemaking, and you come to realize over time that, in putting yourself out there, you're going to deal with both triumph and tragedy, oftentimes in equal measure.

> In putting yourself out there, you're going to deal with both triumph and tragedy, oftentimes in equal measure.

Our city of Augusta, likewise, has had its share of triumphs and tragedies. Unfortunately, over time it had also developed a reputation for race-based politics. Our local government is comprised of eight commission districts along with two super districts, with the mayor being the only official to be elected at large. In 1996, our city and county governments were consolidated, driven by the fact that the city was on the verge of bankruptcy due to fiscal mismanagement. In what was ultimately a shotgun wedding, the voters approved establishing a government that, at the time, pretty much ensured five of the commission seats would be held by African Americans while five would be held by white representatives, with the mayor voting only in the event of a tie. In essence, our current local government was founded upon mistrust, which tends to breed mistrust, as it put commissioners in a situation where they often feel the need to consider the needs of their districts above the needs of the city as a whole. Needless to say, operating under this form of government led to very messy politics, which often gave the appearance of being racially motivated.

Earlier that year, I had gone through a program called Leadership Georgia, which is one of the oldest statewide leadership programs in the nation. The week of my graduation that November, we had our third current or former elected official go under indictment. A friend of mine, Eric Tanenblatt, who was then Governor Sonny Perdue's chief of staff, asked me when I got off the bus in Thomasville, Georgia that Thursday, "What are you guys putting in the water up there?"

That really was the straw that broke the camel's back. I decided at that moment we needed new leadership, and if an office came open, I was going to run for it. I had spent the past year traveling the state and having people ask me, "What's wrong with Augusta politics?" It just infuriated me to hear people have such a bad impression of the city I loved and call home. The city that James Brown called home and that other notable figures like Amy Grant, Charles Kelley and Dave Haywood of Lady Antebellum, Laurence Fishburne, Jessye Norman, and Hulk Hogan came from. The city that serves as the final resting place for two of the signers of the Declaration of Independence and where Ty Cobb got his start in baseball. The city probably best known outside of Georgia as the host of the Masters golf tournament each spring.

In May of 2005, our mayor at the time, Bob Young, announced that he had accepted an appointment by President George W. Bush to become the regional director for the Atlanta region of the US Department of Housing and Urban Development. It was also announced that a special election would be held that November, providing me the opportunity I was looking for to offer myself for public service.

When I decided to run for mayor, I was actually called into a back room, albeit not a smoky one, by a group of business leaders that I knew well—people I still know well and like very much to this day. But I was told not to run, that I certainly would be the best mayor out of the candidates in the field, but I had not paid my dues. Being very competitive, I got angry and said, "Look, I'm gonna run and I'm gonna win if your candidate's in the field or not." And that's exactly what I did, buoyed by the unwavering support of a core group of energetic twenty- and thirtysomething year-olds, who had *virtually no clue* how to run a political campaign.

I announced my run in June of 2005. Eight days later, we lost my mother-in-law, Kitty. Having lost my own mother at an early age, Kitty had become like a second mother to me, and the loss hit our family hard. I remember asking my wife, Malisa, and her dad, Bruz, if they were okay with me continuing on with the campaign. They said, "Augusta needs you, and Kitty would have wanted you to run." Having to run a race dealing with your own grief and the grief of your family is not an easy thing, but that's one thing about leadership: it's never easy.

> Having to run a race dealing with your own grief and the grief of your family is not an easy thing, but that's one thing about leadership: it's never easy.

At the time I threw my hat in the ring for mayor of Augusta, I was at the helm of a very successful nonprofit organization: The Central Savannah River Land Trust. I remember people would ask, "Why do you want to get mixed up in all that?" And I would reply, "Because if everybody takes that attitude, nothing's ever gonna change." I was actually told by a potential supporter over lunch that the idea of trying to unite people around a political campaign with a focus on putting public service above politics sounded *radical.* For me, the idea of public service with regard to offering oneself for a period of time without focusing on a career in politics was one of the founding principles of our nation. Radical? She then went on to tell me that what I was saying sounded too "common sense" and that common sense had no place in politics.

I shared with her my firm belief that common sense should have a seat at *every* table where a decision-making process takes place.

The fact is, change requires a leap of faith. And leading a change takes a competitive nature, and it takes empathy. I'd say that's always been the most frustrating thing to me regarding politics. Human lives are impacted by decisions made by elected officials, and I could see areas of the city that had been long neglected and that desperately needed help—yet had often been used as political footballs. The real problems were never truly addressed in any meaningful way. I remember watching the vice presidential candidates debate in the 2004 election. At that point in time, a great friend of mine—a teacher in an inner-city school—had been nominated for teacher of the year, and she had often told me what she had to deal with in the classroom within the context of a broken education system. I remember hearing one of the vice presidential candidates say, "Well, these are the three bullet points that are going to fix the educational system." And I thought, "Go spend time with my friend in her classroom, and tell *her* that there are three bullet points that are actually going to fix the American education system."

I decided that if I was going to run, I wanted to be a candidate whom people could get excited about. Somebody who didn't use rhetoric or soundbites to try to get elected, because the solutions to fixing our communities or our businesses or our nation are just not as simple as three bullet points. I knew that true authority and influence in today's world are earned, whereas power is *taken*. True leaders understand that their authority and influence are

> The fact is, change requires a leap of faith. And leading a change takes a competitive nature, and it takes empathy.

gifts to be shared, not power to be hoarded and wielded for a finite period of time.

---

I knew that true authority and influence in today's world are earned, whereas power is *taken*. True leaders understand that their authority and influence are gifts to be shared, not power to be hoarded and wielded for a finite period of time.

I presented myself as an alternative to the politics of the status quo by never going negative and running on a track record of unifying leadership. And I'm proud to say I was able to win three elections with 57, 65, and 64 percent of the vote, respectively, and serve the great city of Augusta for nine years. But it wasn't always easy, and here's an illustration of the political climate I entered into.

On December 6, 2005 I won my first race in a runoff and was sworn in the following Monday. My first full commission meeting fell on December 20th, less than a week before Christmas. Through the years, the racial divide on the commission had led to a situation where commissioners would often trade votes to get the six votes necessary to pass a motion. At that point, the five white commissioners were trying to fire Teresa Smith, an African American serving as the director of our department of engineering. At the same time there was a movement afoot to get a gentleman by the name of Howard "Bubba" Willis, who was white and served as the interim head of our fire department, appointed as fire chief. Ultimately, both motions—to fire Teresa and to hire Bubba—were passed with six votes in a meeting that was attended by a standing-room-only crowd and became so heated that the African-

American commissioner who voted to fire Ms. Smith and hire Mr. Willis had to be escorted from the building by our local marshal's department. Through my trial by fire in that first meeting, I realized from the start that in order to be a Changemaker, I was also going to have to be a peacemaker as well. Welcome to local government, Mr. Copenhaver.

In spite of the politically toxic environment I was entering into, I saw hope in my grassroots engagement efforts through years spent serving on the boards of multiple nonprofits. I saw our community at eye level and witnessed firsthand the amazing work unsung individuals were doing daily to improve the lives of their fellow citizens. These efforts crossed all political, racial, social demographic, and geographic lines. I saw people from all walks of life who believed in our city and our community as a whole—rolling up their sleeves and getting their hands dirty on a daily basis to make a difference—and I was inspired by them to do the same thing in a run for elected office. I knew that, in spite of the politics, people loved our city and were proud to call it home. In the end, I simply knew in my heart from engaging our citizens at the grassroots level that people would respond to changemaking leadership if they were provided an alternative to the status quo of politics as usual.

Out of the gates, I got directly involved in economic development and job creation. I'm still very passionate about those issues, because, to me, providing jobs and opportunities to people throughout the community is the great equalizer. I'm proud to have been directly involved in bringing major economic developments into town, like the Fortune 300 company ADP in my first year alone, adding a thousand jobs to our local economy. I also helped bring in a Starbucks manufacturing facility, which was a $172-million-dollar investment in the city. I helped to create literally thousands of jobs while in office, but I don't take full credit for any of these accomplishments, because they were all team efforts. No leader can do anything alone, but if you can inspire people to work with you, you can do amazing things.

Those are all great wins. There were some cool moments as well. Having a beer with Cal Ripken Jr. on my back porch when he was my houseguest while in town for an event. Befriending James Brown and his family and getting to know what a truly special man he was. Honoring Fuzzy Zoeller during his final Masters Tournament. Honoring Lady Antebellum with their own day to recognize our hometown heroes' impact on the world of music. And having a cameo as an assistant coach opposite Lou Holtz in *The Blind Side*—and seeing Sandra Bullock wearing one of my campaign t-shirts.

But the thing I'm proudest of is to hear—now that I'm out of office—that I brought the community together. That was very intentional. The three focus points I had in the forefront of my mind at all times were *healing the racial divide, fostering economic development and job creation*, and *creating a more efficient government*. And it's the first one that dramatically helps with the other two.

> No leader can do anything alone, but if you can inspire people to work with you, you can do amazing things.

> The three focus points I had in the forefront of my mind at all times were *healing the racial divide, fostering economic development and job creation*, and *creating a more efficient government*.

But what if I had listened to my colleagues and just gone with the status quo? What if I thought, "Well, I guess I should give up because we need somebody who has paid their dues."

The fact is, true leadership insists on a constant rejection of the status quo. True leaders demand continuous reflection and improvement of those around them, and even more importantly, of themselves. True leaders are *Changemakers*.

So, what is a Changemaker? It's somebody who's not afraid to do something different in the service of a good cause. Someone who can spark a movement that others can't help but rally around. Changemakers aren't perfect; they're not saints. They're just people like you and me who are willing to roll up their sleeves and get their hands dirty. A Changemaker is someone like Dr. Martin Luther King Jr., a hero of mine. He didn't have a leadership title. He wasn't a CEO or a senator or a president or a pope. But he used his power to inspire others to rally around a common cause to forever change the face of the United States in the name of unity and equality.

Never before has true leadership been needed more than right now in today's uncertain world. Yet as I often say: you don't need a title to lead. Whether you're a CEO of a Fortune 500 company or just starting to build a business, whether you're embarking on a foray into public service or have spent a lifetime in politics, whether you're a single parent trying to

## You don't need a title to lead.

make ends meet or a widow crusading for a cause you're passionate about, you are a leader. But *true* leadership requires becoming a Changemaker.

It was all my lessons in life and in leadership that provided the inspiration for this book. I firmly believe, to realize the potential in ourselves and our communities, both the leaders of today and the next generation of leaders need to reject the status quo and become Changemakers.

*The Changemaker: The Art of Building Better Leaders* is a road map of sorts, designed to deliver comprehensive, common-sense leadership strategies to people from all walks of life. Through personal and professional anecdotes, case studies, and the wisdom from Changemakers gone by, I will inspire and empower you to embrace adversity, rely on creativity and character, and sometimes take the road less traveled in order to unlock your ultimate potential.

Helping to build better leaders is truly an art, as it takes creativity, patience, persistence, and a diligent focus on releasing the potential of any canvas set before you in your leadership endeavors. This book is dedicated to helping you to further develop your inner-Changemaker by taking a deep-dive into what I call the Seven Attributes of Changemakers:

> Helping to build better leaders is truly an art, as it takes creativity, patience, persistence, and a diligent focus on releasing the potential of any canvas set before you in your leadership endeavors.

1.  **Creativity**—rejecting the status quo and embarking in uncharted territory, exploring creative solutions to problems.

2.  **Courage**—rising to the occasion in the face of adversity.

3.  **Connecting**—unifying the masses and rallying around a common cause.

4. **Listening**—embracing others' points of view, hearing/ respecting what others have to say.

5. **Transparency**—always remaining open, authentic, realizing the power in vulnerability.

6. **Composure**—maintaining a sense of calm and duty when chaos ensues.

7. **Character**—demonstrating a consistent sense of ethics and moral compass in all actions.

Let's face it, change is inevitable. You learn to pivot, adapt, and embrace it … or you get run over by it. Changemakers, however, *want* to see a change in the world. They work to inspire others to want to rally around their vision, around the common purpose and a higher cause, to really impact positive change for generations to come, and to build better leaders.

You've just taken your first step to becoming a Changemaker!

Happy reading!

chapter one

# The Outsider

*To have a positive and lasting impact as an insider, it's important
to have a true appreciation of what it feels like to be an outsider.*

**—DEKE COPENHAVER**

I could just imagine the headline: *Storm of the Century Crushes Augusta
While Mayor Relaxes on Florida Beach*. It was Tuesday, February 11,
2014, and I had just walked off a stage in Orlando, Florida after
speaking at the Philips Healthcare Mega Meeting. Al Dallas, my
executive assistant, informed me that all flights back to Atlanta had
been canceled, so getting back home to Augusta by air was not an
option.

Having watched as Snowmageddon crippled Atlanta just two weeks earlier, along with the subsequent reaction to the response of elected officials by both the public and the media, I knew that being stuck in Florida in the face of a crisis of that magnitude would not be a good thing. I also knew that not getting back was *not* an option, as the people I served needed me more than ever. As Al and I quickly got a handle on the situation, we agreed that there was only one choice left: rent a car.

Fortunately, the weather for the drive back had not yet deteriorated, so the trip went very smoothly. Thank the Lord for Al being at the wheel, as it provided two great benefits: Al is a much faster driver than I am, so he got us back quicker than I ever would have. Plus, riding shotgun allowed me to stay on all my devices to closely monitor the situation along the way.

During the drive back, I was informed that Jim Cantore from The Weather Channel was in town and was looking to get an interview from me. They say you know things are really, really bad from a weather perspective when Jim shows up. But ever being an optimist, I figured it was a good thing. I could give my citizens an idea of the gravity of the situation and the need for them to hunker down and stay off the roads, which I'd learned was half the battle in dealing with weather events like this one.

When I finally arrived back home that evening, I charged up my iPad and phones and set up a makeshift control center in my kitchen to stay on top of the situation and in constant contact with the fire chief, the city administrator, our sheriff, our traffic engineer, representatives of Georgia Power, and other key personnel who were on the front lines of dealing with the storm. By 11:30 p.m., our fire chief, Chris James, brought the paperwork for me to sign to declare a state of emergency.

Needless to say, it was a long night. I set out the next morning to meet The Weather Channel for a live interview. By that time, most roads were becoming impassable. Fortunately, I had Steve Cassell, our lead traffic engineer, to guide me as I drove downtown to the news crew's makeshift headquarters at the Marriott. This would be one of my last shots to connect with my city, to be seen, before the major power outages that were on the way made tuning into local broadcasts impossible. I knew I needed to reassure our citizens that we were as prepared as we could be for a natural disaster like this, while encouraging them once again to stay inside and stay off the roads.

Throughout the day, conditions began to deteriorate with the worst to come that evening. I continued to monitor the situation and remained in constant contact with our team and with the governor's office, keeping them informed on how things were playing out locally. As the power outages began to take hold, I took to Twitter to relay the most accurate, up-to-date information to our local citizens. That evening was one I'll never forget. As I looked out over my backyard, I was mesmerized watching trees being snapped like twigs, seeing transformers blowing into splashes of green light, lending an other-worldly atmosphere to the skies over the city.

The next morning, I was notified that Governor Nathan Deal, a friend, a statesman, and a changemaking leader, would be coming by helicopter to tour the damage, and he wanted me to accompany him. I remember looking out my front window and seeing nothing but downed trees, thinking there was no way I could get to the airport. Fortunately, one of the most inspiring responses I witnessed during this harrowing event was the way our community came together, neighbors helping neighbors. Whether it was providing food and shelter or forming chainsaw crews to clear neighborhood streets, the way our citizens responded is something I'll never forget. A group of friends ultimately cleared a path out of my neighborhood, and I was able to meet the governor and tour the damage.

The ensuing cleanup was massive and certainly no easy task. We even had an earthquake that Friday evening which served to rattle a few more nerves, my own included, in a community that had just weathered the storm of the century. Despite the damage, there was a silver lining in the disaster: there was no loss of life. And I will always believe that the way our community came together represents our finest hour.

I use this event to illustrate the importance of leaders having a presence in a time of crisis, connecting with others—essentially *being seen and having a presence*—is a critical aspect of a Changemaker. In every single capacity that I served and worked, I always made it a point to be seen and to have a presence. But it wasn't always that way. Believe it or not, when I was young, I was an outsider with no interest in being seen.

In fact, I wanted to be invisible.

## A Canadian Kid in the Deep South

My parents intended to have four kids, each two years apart. First, they had my oldest brother, Andy, and two years later my sister,

Paula. Then about four years after that they had my brother, John. My sister, Lisa, came as a bit of a surprise twelve years after John. Mom grew up as an only child and just couldn't stand the thought of Lisa being lonely. So, although she was over forty at that point, she went to the doctor and asked, "Would it be safe for me to try for another child?" He said, "Well, if you didn't have any problem with that one, you'll probably be okay." So, I guess you could say I was conceived with a destiny of service to others, since my initial purpose in life was to keep my sister company.

As the youngest of five children, I spent my early years in Montreal, where my father was the vice president of a major chemical company called Celanese. When I was about four years old, he was offered the position as CEO of a company in New York as well as one in Chicago. He had actually purchased a house in Chicago in anticipation of taking that particular job, when suddenly a position in Augusta came open for president and CEO of Columbia Nitrogen, a subsidiary of Dutch State Mining, headquartered in the Netherlands. My parents really didn't like the idea of us growing up in a big city, so we moved to Augusta.

Talk about culture shock. A kid with a thick Canadian accent suddenly transplanted in the heart of the Deep South. I just wanted to disappear. I was so shy that I cried the first day of kindergarten, just terrified to go to school and be around other kids. I was even too shy to go to birthday parties. I was invited to plenty of them, but I don't think I ever attended a single one. I believe it was somewhere around fifth grade that my sister, Lisa, gave me some advice to overcome my shyness. She told me that girls liked guys who drew attention to themselves by getting into trouble. Not exactly the soundest advice, but it was a start … and to her credit she was correct, which would lead me to more than my share of scrapes with trouble during my formative years. I can honestly say I bet my parents wished Lisa had held her tongue on that one.

## The Power of Connecting

Shyness can often be misinterpreted as arrogance. And for a painfully shy kid, being perceived as arrogant just makes it that much more difficult. Whether it was my accent or my silence, I always felt like an outsider, as if I was constantly being judged. On top of it, I grew up in a bedroom community adjacent to Augusta, Columbia County. Today, it has become an affluent bedroom community, but that definitely wasn't always the case. Back then, many people pictured everybody who lived in Columbia County as rednecks. Although we lived in a nice neighborhood, that didn't stop many people who lived in Augusta proper from basically painting with a broad brush and assigning unpleasant labels to people who lived on my side of the county line. I learned then and there how it felt to be prejudged based solely on where you lived. And in all fairness, the painting with a broad brush, labeling, and pre-judging went both ways in my youth, as there were many people in my neck of the woods who thought everyone in Augusta proper was born with a silver spoon their mouths and an axe to grind against people from our part of town, which was absolutely not the case. Having ultimately developed friendships with people on both sides of the county line, it was

> It was impressed upon me at a young age that stereotyping people by where they live or who they choose to hang out with is never a wise course of action, because people never fit easily into a basket.

impressed upon me at a young age that stereotyping people by where they live or who they choose to hang out with is never a wise course of action, because people never fit easily into a basket.

I learned some valuable lessons from my father when he hosted cocktail parties at the house. Despite my shyness, he made me stand at the front door and greet everyone as they arrived. Particularly, when we'd have the Dutch people from his company in town, I had the chance to meet and interact with people of all different cultures, which tremendously broadened my horizons. It primed me for being a little more social and interacting with people who were *perceived* as different. And I learned quickly, they weren't so different after all. As I got older, I developed a great appreciation for different cultures and the importance of inclusion.

And I realized the importance of connecting with others, which (contrary to my sister's troublemaking advice) ultimately became the antidote to my shyness. I was a voracious reader. I loved music and sports and just wanted to learn everything I could about all the different passions I had. Partly because I loved to learn, but also because I knew that if I could speak with some sort of authority or genuine interest on a whole range of topics, it made it easier to connect. I knew I could find something in common with whomever I would meet.

Ironically, it was my shyness that emotionally tied me to others and allowed me to open up. It kept me sensitive to others' feelings and sincere in my own—another characteristic of true leadership and of a Changemaker. Today I'm comfortable getting up and speaking in front of thousands of people, because I know deep down that I could get any one of those audience members in a room, one on one, and connect with them. My shyness provided my emotional connection to people, and particularly to people who feel like their needs haven't been met or their voices haven't been heard.

> My shyness provided my emotional connection to people, and particularly to people who feel like their needs haven't been met or their voices haven't been heard.

The first time I ever spoke in a church was in 2005, when I first ran for mayor. I was actually a deacon in my own church at that time, but I was invited to speak at Macedonia Baptist, an African-American church. That experience was life-changing for me, because I felt more comfortable speaking there than at any gala affair. I knew what it meant to feel like an outsider, to feel excluded, to feel prejudged, and to go unheard. I just understood. And that campaign season, I'm proud and humbled to say, I was invited to speak in many African-American churches—because they felt what I felt: a connection.

## My Father's Head, My Mother's Heart

My father was a man of few words. He was not overly verbose, so much so that when he went on a hunting trip once with country musician Roy Clark from *Hee Haw*, Roy nicknamed my father the Professor. Because, according to Roy, "he doesn't say much, but when he has something to say, you listen." Dad was a great golfer, very competitive. He was a great shot when hunting, and he loved the outdoors, having been raised on a farm for the better part of his childhood. Just a very solid guy and truly a southern gentleman, well-loved with a great heart.

My appreciation for the military comes from my father. He was seventeen when he joined up and flew B-17 bombers in World War II. Having lost his own father at the age of twelve and being raised one of five children by a single mother who was a teacher during the Great Depression, so much of what he learned about being a man, he learned during his military service: such as the values of honor, integrity, and duty.

My mother was a sweet southern lady. She was funny. She loved her kids and her grandkids. She never worked outside the house, being a stay-at-home mom. She had dreamed of becoming a nurse, and I knew sometimes that bothered her. But I used to tell her, "You know, Mom, raising five kids is a job in and of itself." She loved to garden and to play bridge, and she was very socially outgoing. I couldn't have asked for a better mother.

Interestingly though, my father was a Republican, while my mother was a Democrat. I suppose that's what influenced me to become politically Independent, having served as such during my time in office. I often say I inherited my father's head and my mother's heart.

Our political climate today is more divided, more polarized than it's ever been. It's increasingly disturbing to hear some of the rhetoric being spewed across cable news channels and social media, from both sides of the aisle. So much hate and anger and, sadly, violence over political affiliations and differing ideologies. It was never that way in my home.

Every night at the dinner table, at some point, politics would be discussed. My parents, even though they disagreed politically, had a standing policy to never go to bed angry. And they were married for well over forty years, during which they never voted for the same presidential candidate. I think they actually enjoyed the political discourse, the challenge in trying to get the other to come over to their point of view. Yet despite differing opinions, I saw that they shared the same value system. I think that's from both of them being originally from and raised in small towns in Virginia. The value system that they had with regard to the family was always the common ground. As my father aged, he became a little bit more mellow on social issues, but it was a marriage that worked and produced five kids, ten grandchildren, and eleven great-grandchildren.

Rather than being skewed one way or the other, that healthy discourse taught me to look at things from all angles. I think political parties all too often focus on the two or three issues that divide us, when most people want in life are to live in clean, safe communities, have access to education for their children, and have access to jobs and opportunities and good health care. I learned that as a child at the dinner table.

> Rather than being skewed one way or the other, that healthy discourse taught me to look at things from all angles.

The key is to learn to listen without prejudice. Observe and be willing to learn. If you're immediately going to go on the defensive about something, how are you ever going to get to resolution? Being a shy kid and sitting at the dinner table just listening, soaking it all in, that planted the seeds of my negotiating skills as a Changemaker.

## Coming Full Circle

I've been in banking, real estate and development, I ran a nonprofit, a land-conservation organization, I was mayor of a major city for nine years and a radio show host. Today I'm principal of Copenhaver

Consulting, a growing niche consulting firm here in Augusta. In every position, the subplot for me has been *connecting*.

As a shy kid from Montreal, I never would have thought any of this would have been possible. Speaking before thousands at the

> In every position, the subplot for me has been *connecting*.

Philips Healthcare Mega Conference in Orlando, or for the International Association of Outsourcing Professionals World Summit in Phoenix. Appearing multiple times on The Weather Channel, or on CNN and the BBC, or more times than I can count on our local news station affiliates. Starring in the movie *Forces of Nature* with Ben Affleck and Sandra Bullock (okay, maybe not *starring* as there's currently no Oscar for "Best Extra in a Non-Speaking Role"), and playing the assistant coach for Lou Holtz in *The Blind Side*.

The ability to connect and communicate is critical for a leader, and for a Changemaker. In my core, I really want to reach people. In fact, my TEDx Talk title was *Cities: Where All Things Connect*. I just love the power of community. To me, everything is a community, whether it's a business or a neighborhood or a social movement.

Speaking now just comes naturally to me, I'm comfortable in the spotlight. I don't make notes. I don't use teleprompters. I always speak extemporaneously. I don't even like to use PowerPoints, because I like to paint pictures with words. As a leader, if you're speaking unscripted, people know that it's coming from the heart, so you connect with your audience no matter who it is or where it is. I can just feel the connection with my audience when I'm speaking. Ultimately, in speaking from the heart you develop the rhythm and the timing akin to a musician's connection to an audience in memorable musical moments.

Take it from someone who was once a shy kid from Canada, there is immense power in the human voice. There's no better way for a leader to engage people than speaking to them directly. The power of being a Changemaker comes in taking every opportunity you can to speak to others. When people get to know you, they begin to trust you.

> As a leader, if you're speaking unscripted, people know that it's coming from the heart, so you connect with your audience no matter who it is or where it is.

And when they trust you, real change begins.

## Lose the Script

We've all seen it before. A business leader, politician or some other public figure looks directly into a camera and tries to sincerely deliver a message from a teleprompter or from another pre-approved script. Sometimes it comes off without a hitch. Sometimes it's so bad that it makes us squirm inside. More often than not, the last thing it comes off as is authentic and believable with the outcome having very little real impact on the targeted audience. But it doesn't have to be that way, if you're willing to do one thing: open up and speak from your heart.

In leadership positions, it's just a simple fact that at some point you're going to have to deliver a message through a camera to a mass audience, to a group of employees or to an audience with a very short attention span that doesn't want to hear you drone on all day. Always remember that what you say doesn't have to come off sounding like a soundbite or a speech that's been scripted and rehearsed, which is exactly what words that have been written for you, edited, and re-edited come off sounding like unless you're an extraordinarily gifted communicator. If you really want to connect with your audience, whoever and wherever they may be, don't be afraid to go off script every now and again or even consider throwing the script out the window altogether. As scary as it may be for some of us to speak unscripted in any setting, I can tell you firsthand that it works—for one simple reason. When your words are unscripted there's no doubt in your audience's mind whose words you're speaking: they're yours.

I've often shared with people that sincerity is something which can't be faked and is something that builds a bond of trust between you and your audience that is hard to break. Speaking in an extemporaneous, unscripted fashion also serves to connect you with your audience in another way, in that it's like walking a tightrope without a net. Not relying on a teleprompter or a script in today's world is a bit unusual, and it has the tendency to hold your audience's attention due to the very real fact that you could stumble and fall flat on your face at any given moment.

Call it living dangerously if you will, but being a Changemaker requires an edge of authenticity.

Call it living dangerously if you will, but being a Changemaker requires an edge of authenticity.

## TWO CENTS FOR CHANGE

In today's world, the art of communication in many ways has become a dying art. People are constantly bombarded with messages vying for their attention at an ever-increasing rate. The ability for leaders to deliver clear and concise messages that move and motivate people through a haze of misinformation is now more critical than ever. Knowing how to set your message apart is an absolute key to success in any endeavor you undertake.

Messages delivered sincerely and from the heart may not be as catchy as the latest YouTube video, but they do one thing much better than any canned or contrived message will ever do: they resonate with your audience in a way that both touches their hearts and causes them to think. And that's what sets such messages apart.

1.  As a potential Changemaker, have you ever tried delivering an unscripted and unrehearsed message to the people you serve? It may come as a shock to some, but most of Dr. Martin Luther King Jr.'s "I Have A Dream" speech was improvised.

2.  As a potential Changemaker, when was the last time you chose to purposely get outside your comfort zone in an effort to deliver your message to a crowd or organization you may think is unresponsive to your vision? I've always found that a good rule of thumb is that if you can make an audience laugh, you're halfway towards bringing them around.

3.  In a leadership position, have you purposely attempted to interact with and develop an understanding of different

cultures impacted by your efforts to promote positive change? During my time in office, I made it a point to attend as many culturally diverse events as possible as it helped build a strong connection with sectors of the community who often felt underrepresented.

4.  In a leadership position, when is the last time you fully and purposefully considered both sides of an argument before making a final decision without letting emotion weigh too heavily in the process? In today's world where everything seems to be so immediate, I've always found the old carpentry saying "measure twice, cut once" can best be employed by patiently and attentively considering both sides of an issue before making a final decision, leading to better decision-making in the long run.

5.  As a potential Changemaker, have you ever purposely made a decision which may have been unpopular and gone against the status quo simply because you knew it was the right thing to do? While serving in office, I was faced with having to vote to break a tie for a tax increase. Although I knew voting in favor of it wouldn't be popular, I also knew that employees had not been given raises in five years and that the mileage rate had not been increased in seven years. Though there was some initial blowback, the news cycle moved on quickly and I knew in my heart I'd made the right decision for our employees as well as our community as a whole.

chapter two

# What Kind of a
# Leader Are You?

*As a student of leadership, I've learned that great leadership
means, at its core, always leading from a good heart.*

**—DEKE COPENHAVER**

In 2010, the US was at the height of the recession. Businesses were
suffering, communities were suffering, and families were suffering. A
local news anchor who happened to be a friend of mine mentioned
that somewhere in the neighborhood of $2 billion had been spent
the prior election cycle for political campaign ads, where half the

people lost anyway. So, when I announced I'd be running again for mayor, I really put some thought into it. How much waste did I have in my first two campaigns? Did I really need to go with the flow and hire consultants to win? Did I really want to raise the capital for thousands of political mailers that likely would just end up in the trash?

I had to decide if I wanted to campaign to win ... or *lead* to win. With the financial climate as it was, I knew that local nonprofits and families and individuals needed money more than I did. The old song "If You Don't Know Me By Now" came to mind, and I thought after serving Augusta for five years, the good citizens of the city were either satisfied with me as their mayor or they weren't.

> I had to decide if I wanted to campaign to win ... or *lead* to win.

I didn't consult with anybody before I made such an unorthodox move, because it was just the right thing to do. In what was counterintuitive to "politics as usual," I asked people to give to local charities as opposed to giving to my campaign. We ran the campaign on about $5,000 in a city with a population of two hundred thousand residents. We didn't do any TV ads. We didn't do any mail-outs. And as far as I was aware, we ran the only carbon-neutral major campaign ever seen in the US, because we asked any supporters who posted yard signs to recycle them at the end.

I stuck to my message: healing the racial divide, fostering economic development and job creation, and focusing on better governmental efficiency. While other politicians drowned their audience in platitudes, I provided clear and concise measurables— the number of jobs created, or the amount of corporate investment in the community. I would always reference the monthly Mayor's

Prayer Breakfast we started my first day in office and discuss the hope I saw, and the progress made with regard to the community coming together. And then I'd give evidence of the continued drive toward a more efficient government.

The results? We won with 64 percent of the vote.

## Finding Common Ground

How was I able to win by such a large majority of not only votes but also the hearts and minds of Augusta's citizens? True leaders, Changemakers that is, connect with people by finding common ground.

The vast majority of people I talk to are simply good, everyday men and women living and working and raising families in communities across our nation. And we are all unified around several principles

> True leaders, Changemakers that is, connect with people by finding common ground.

which, although often hijacked by politics, serve as common ground.

In my very unscientific information-gathering technique of having simple conversations with people I meet from all walks of life, I've found (as mentioned in the previous chapter) that we are not so different: we want to live in communities that are safe, we want the ability to educate our children, and we want opportunities for good-paying jobs and access to sufficient health care. How cities go about creating a culture that provides for these common-ground opportunities can be open for debate. The realization by local governments that the citizens we serve, no matter the district they live in, and are not too dissimilar when it comes to their basic wants and needs, can provide a framework for leaders from all walks of life to work together toward resolving big-picture issues facing cities nationwide.

I was reminded of the power of seeking common ground when I had the pleasure of recently serving as the keynote speaker for Augusta University's fourth annual Junior Model United Nations at the invitation of my friend, Dr. Craig Albert. The event was attended by 150 middle school students from eleven schools in the Augusta area. During the session, students were designated as delegates representing more than fifty countries. Their focus was on one very relevant issue to our community and to the nation: cyber security. The group was remarkably diverse, with students representing different regions, faiths, ethnicities, genders, and socioeconomic backgrounds.

The premise of the event revolved around the Model UN Security Council being charged with the responsibility of regaining control of NORAD, the North American missile-defense agency, after the agency was successfully hacked by North Korea. The students, as delegates for their designated nation, were challenged to come up with a directive and action to avert the crisis by keeping North Korea from selling the information they had acquired through the hack. An intense situation for a group of middle schoolers to say the least!

What I witnessed in the room where the students were gathered was nothing short of inspirational. The delegates were able to work together, to agree to disagree, to compromise, and ultimately to resolve the conflict they'd been faced with. In a matter of hours, these middle schoolers were able to come to a common-ground solution to the problem while listening to each other's often opposing viewpoints, all the while treating each other with dignity and respect. Throughout the day, new friendships were formed, and a comradery was developed among the 150 students, many of whom had not met prior to the event.

I was overwhelmed and encouraged to see how a group of young people could set aside their differences and work together toward the solution of a big-picture issue with a focus on serving the greater good.

You can undoubtedly learn a lot by watching and listening to younger generations. Those were young leaders, young Changemakers, indeed.

## Pandering Is an Extreme Sport

As a leader, is it possible to make everybody happy? Not by a long shot.

> I was overwhelmed and encouraged to see how a group of young people could set aside their differences and work together toward the solution of a big-picture issue with a focus on serving the greater good.

Before I had decided whether I would run for mayor, I ended up going on our church leadership retreat. At that time, I was serving on the board of deacons at Reid Memorial Presbyterian Church. Sometime during the retreat, the moderator made the point that, in church politics, you have 3 percent of the people who are for everything … and they're very vocal about it. Then you have 3 percent who are against everything, and they're quite vocal, too. You also have 12 percent who are for everything, but not so loud. And another 12 percent who are against, but not so loud. And, finally, you have the 70 percent in the middle. If you're

> If you're governing to the loud sides of the spectrum, then you're not doing what's right for the majority of the people you serve.

governing to the loud sides of the spectrum, then you're not doing what's right for the majority of the people you serve.

That was my focus on governing. True leadership means you just can't be everything to everybody. Of course, that philosophy occasionally got me in trouble with the extremes. At one point I was targeted by a group called Georgia Gun Owners because I had joined a group called Mayors Against Illegal Guns. I mean, who *wouldn't* be against illegal guns, right? That's just common sense.

Unbeknownst to me, however, the group I had joined had been started by Michael Bloomberg and on a national stage was rather controversial. The Georgia Gun Owners organization labeled me as an anti-gun mayor and put out a statewide email for people to call and express their displeasure with me. Though the extreme group claimed to have twenty thousand members, I probably received around a hundred total calls or emails. I took each call and explained that I'm a gun owner myself. I grew up hunting. I'm still a hunter, and I take offense to being labeled as being anti-gun. I faced the extreme head on, and the situation dissipated.

In another incident several weeks later, I received a letter from the Freedom from Religion Foundation demanding that we cease and desist the Mayor's Prayer Breakfast, because we were allegedly violating the separation of church and state. However, there were no city resources spent. It was the churches that hosted and offered breakfast at absolutely no expense to the city. Ultimately, we just renamed it the Augusta Community Prayer Breakfast and the extremists

Changemakers may be attacked by the extremes at times, but all that means is that you're effectively serving the silent majority.

went away ... with the breakfast still going strong today thirteen years after it began!

Changemakers may be attacked by the extremes at times, but all that means is that you're effectively serving the silent majority.

## Current State of Leadership

In surveying the landscape of leadership today, I am truly concerned. Our news is filled with political leaders trying to win at all costs by making people afraid of the other side. Conscienceless mudslinging. Dividing as opposed to uniting. Using manipulation and fear-mongering to retain and increase their own power base or the power base of the organizations they serve.

We have corporate leaders who forego environmental safety, ethics, and humanity just to pad the bottom line. CEOs who serve their own interests as opposed to serving the hard-working people in their company. And barely a day goes by that we don't see the blatant abuse of power of those in positions of authority, sworn to protect the community.

I don't want to paint with too broad a brush here, because there are, without a doubt, great, inspirational leaders out there. I have friends in politics and who lead companies who are good people, and I see examples of leadership in our communities every day.

Nonprofit leaders work tirelessly in service to their organizations' missions; civic-minded business leaders make philanthropy a priority; school administrators care for our children; teachers pay for supplies out of their own pockets; leaders within police departments willingly put their lives on the line every day. There are leaders in the less than 1 percent of our nation's population who volunteer themselves and their families for military service to protect our freedoms daily and leaders in our neighborhoods—parents and grandparents and aunts and uncles.

As I stated in the last chapter, you don't need a title to be a leader. Leadership is not based on age, race, political affiliation, religion, income, or gender. It's based on *leading*. Just making the effort to be a good role model, a selfless, compassionate human being whom others can learn from, suddenly catapults you into a position of leadership.

> As I stated in the last chapter, you don't need a title to be a leader. Leadership is not based on age, race, political affiliation, religion, income, or gender. It's based on *leading*.

But what's the difference between leading and being a *great* leader?

## Defining True Leadership

True leadership is not about power and control. Leadership is about making people feel safe, included, heard, respected, and protected. I think that's where we as a society have gone a little awry on the definition and execution of leadership.

Not long ago, I was talking to a friend of mine about the alpha in a pack of wolves. He said, "People think about the alpha a certain way—the top dog, the dominator. But alpha in the animal kingdom is the protector of the pack, the protector of the family, the protector of the community."

True leaders are just average human beings who are willing to step out in faith and oftentimes simply do what no one else wants to do. They have the ability to inspire others through their words, but more than that, through their actions. They walk it like they talk it. Dr. Martin Luther King, Jr. went to jail right alongside the people he was leading.

Great leaders don't ask anybody to do anything they wouldn't do themselves. The leaders who I respect are down there in the trenches with the people that they lead. It's easy to have a stage and a microphone and talk about doing something meaningful, but it's not so easy to roll up your sleeves and get your hands dirty and actually make things happen.

> True leaders are just average human beings who are willing to step out in faith and oftentimes simply do what no one else wants to do.

## Becoming a Changemaker

We've all heard the statement from someone around us when we suggest trying something new: "But we've always done it this way!" To this, I defer to the wisdom of Thomas Dewar, Scottish Baron and co-founder of Dewar's Whiskey (my favorite Scotch by the way): "Minds are like parachutes—they only function when open."

I'll be the first to admit that change can be a difficult and often uncomfortable thing to deal with. Whether it be the loss of a loved one, undertaking a new business venture, or a quantum shift in new technologies to keep up with the world, we tend to want to dig in and clutch for dear life at the

> Change is inescapable. And the faster we learn to adjust to it, whether it be in our personal, professional, or civic lives, the easier life becomes.

comfort of the status quo. That being said, change is inescapable. And the faster we learn to adjust to it, whether it be in our personal, professional, or civic lives, the easier life becomes.

Through the years I've often made the point that organizations and communities are either moving forward or moving backwards, as there's simply no standing in place. In a fast-changing world, cities and businesses that are adaptable to change are thriving, while those that continue to adhere to the status quo while being driven by conventional wisdom simply aren't.

An example I've often used regarding adapting to change is the impact of social networking on the world of politics, which was still in its infancy when I was first elected mayor of Augusta in 2005. With its incredible power to sway elections or ignite political scandal, social networking became a way of life in politics, and citizens simply expect their elected officials to have an online presence. Imagine the expense that goes into handling political Twitter and Facebook accounts, an expense and an avenue for information exchange politicians didn't have to concern themselves with only a decade ago. We have yet to see what new technologies will impact both politics and society as a whole in the coming decade, but we can all rest assured that there's more change on the horizon.

In the end, change is inevitable and life is always going to throw us curveballs. Oftentimes in life, success or failure is determined simply by our willingness to embrace change and move beyond conventional wisdom while we learn to hit those curveballs in the process.

So how do you become a Changemaker? There are some basic strategies. Through my time in office, I've come to realize it's impossible to become a Changemaker by pandering/catering to the vocal minority. In order to be a Changemaker, you have to have the discipline to not overly engage these groups, of which there are many, and to understand that there are minds you are never going to change. Ultimately, overly engaging these groups is a waste of precious time and energy and can be akin to arguing with drunks. My policy when confronted by them is to listen politely and then move on.

In order to be a Changemaker, you must be willing to engage people in meaningful conversations "where they are" with those who don't look, think, or act like you. In order to build trusting relationships necessary to implement positive change, Changemakers have to be willing to go beyond their own comfort zones and engage people where *they* feel comfortable. A bar where twenty-somethings hang out, a restaurant in an area you don't usually frequent, the steam room at the YMCA, or the employee lounge for executives are all examples of places where people feel comfortable in sharing their opinions freely.

Changemakers work smart and maximize the use of their time. In order to maximize my time, I found changemaking was made easier through hard-earned, trusting relationships with decision-makers. In order to make change happen at a heightened pace, it helps to have decision-makers on board with your vision.

Changemakers have to translate a vision for whatever audience they're addressing. Changemakers have to understand how to speak many languages and converse with a diverse set of audiences, from business executives and elected officials to neighborhood associations, not to mention your average man/woman on the street from all walks of life.

Finally, vulnerability is a key trait of any Changemaker. Pretending to have all the answers while advancing a goal or a vision comes off as inauthentic, and it creates a sense of mistrust versus a sense of trust around the Changemaker. Admitting that you don't have all the answers and that you need the input and buy-in of a diverse number of individuals and organizations in order to fully bring the vision to life has the opposite effect. Always remember that vulnerability, although often portrayed as a weakness, is actually a tremendous strength, as it takes true courage to honestly open up and face your fears in any given situation.

I'm always reminded of a great example of using vulnerability as a way to connect with your audience when I attend concerts where artists fully interact with the crowd. The Guitar Pull was started here in Augusta twenty years ago and features an all-star lineup of country music artists in a relaxed setting, with everyone seated next to each other on stage with just their guitars. Artists take turns playing songs and telling the stories behind them. In what has become a show not to be missed, the success has largely been driven by the intimate feel of the stars opening up to, and becoming vulnerable to, their audience. The connection with the artists is palpable. Obviously, musicians have known the power of vulnerability since the first chord was ever struck.

There you have it, the core of what defines the Seven Attributes of Changemakers. Here's the list again, which we'll explore in greater detail in the chapters to follow:

1. Creativity

2. Courage

3. Connecting

4. Listening

5. Transparency

6. Composure

7. Character

Now begins your journey to becoming a Changemaker!

**TWO CENTS FOR CHANGE**

Becoming a changemaker is no easy task, as it takes time, discipline, and a willingness to oftentimes go against conventional wisdom. In any leadership position, there can be a temptation to give in to the vocal minority while overlooking the needs of the silent majority. However, becoming a changemaker means having a willingness to find ways to engage with and listen to people from across the spectrum while at the same time challenging the status quo in the process.

1.  As a leader, have you found yourself spending an inordinate amount of time listening to the vocal minority in your spheres of influence and allowing them to play a key role in your decision-making process? Remember, when making decisions in leadership roles, catering to the vocal minority is basically like giving in to children every time they throw a tantrum. You wouldn't want to raise a child like that, and it's definitely not a good way to grow a business or a community as a whole.

2.  In your leadership role, when was the last time you had a meaningful and productive conversation with people you'd never met in a place where they felt comfortable and you may not have? One attribute of great leaders is that they always keep their finger on the pulse of the organizations they serve, and there's no better way of keeping your finger on the pulse than getting outside your comfort zone.

3.  As a potential Changemaker, how many strong working relationships do you have with decision-makers where one call can solve a problem? I can honestly tell you that

in leading positive change in any organization, access to and relationships with decision-makers makes the process that much easier—since we're all in the business, one way or another, of problem-solving. Expediting how quickly you can resolve an issue saves a lot of time and energy you could more profitably be expending somewhere else.

4.  As a potential Changemaker, when was the last time you spoke to or successfully translated your message to an individual, entity, or organization whose goals at first didn't seem to mirror your own, but who ultimately were brought alongside your vision? During my time in office, I was constantly amazed by how much progress could be made by speaking to, and more importantly listening to, individuals and crowds who didn't seem like natural partners in my efforts to promote positive change. I finally realized these individuals and organizations simply wanted to be invited to be a part of the process, and many ended up becoming some of my strongest supporters

5.  As a potential Changemaker, when was the last time you were able to publicly, openly, and honestly share your own vulnerabilities while leading an effort to create positive change? During my first year in office, I was speaking to a Christian alternative school for teenagers when I was asked the question: "Have you ever tried drugs?" I thought about it for a minute in a room full of kids and their parents, and answered, "I wish I could say no, but I can't. But I can tell you that in my lifetime I've seen drugs ruin the lives of a whole lot of my friends, and I've never seen long-term drug use lead anyone to happiness." Afterwards, the parents thanked me for being honest.

chapter three

# Creativity: Take the Road Less Traveled

*There is a true art to being a Changemaker; it begins with the ability to see beyond the boundaries of conventional wisdom and always keeping your eye on the big picture.*

**—DEKE COPENHAVER**

In 2008, the Laney Walker/Bethlehem Revitalization Project had come to loggerheads. We needed just six votes to pass the restoration and revitalization initiative of two historic neighborhoods, Laney Walker and Bethlehem, to regenerate a critical part of Augusta's urban core, yet the ten commissioners of the city couldn't seem to reach common ground.

I knew this was a defining moment for our city. The vote would establish funding strategies for community development in the neighborhoods, to turn around decades of blight and disinvestment, and to rebuild nearly eleven hundred acres of Augusta's urban center by constructing new homes while renovating others. Fortunately, we had a great team assembled in our housing and neighborhood-development department who I knew could implement the plan under with the leadership of director Chester Wheeler, along with our city administrator Fred Russell, a trusted friend and skilled negotiator—both men diligently focusing on successfully moving the project forward. In a latter phase of the development, we were planning to create a Heritage Trail for pedestrians, cyclists, and motorists that would wind through the two neighborhoods while showcasing historic sites for tourists and locals. We wanted to do this so that the prominent African-American businesses and leaders of the past who had shaped the neighborhoods would not be forgotten.

However, one commissioner simply wasn't having it. Earlier, we had been working on the development of a new convention center, and we needed more funding for it. In order to do that, we raised the hotel/motel room fee in the city by $1. But now we had money left over—$38.5 million to be exact—and the dissenting commissioner suggested we put it toward transit. Those commissioners who agreed saw an opportunity to use this as a bargaining chip, in order to ensure six votes that would allow the development of the convention center to proceed. However, the attempted maneuver was not able to manufacture the six votes necessary to move forward.

I've seen this happen in politics too often. You get in the either/or situation. It's a zero-sum game; either we move forward building the new convention center along with allocating the surplus to transit, or the convention center project is stopped in its tracks.

Yet a Changemaker has the ability to look at things from all different sides, to think outside the box, to take the road less traveled, as Robert Frost might say. I knew we had to get creative to keep everything from stalling out. Being very passionate about community redevelopment, I knew there was a commissioner who shared that passion, especially about seeing the Laney Walker and Bethlehem neighborhoods redeveloped. She'd grown up in them. After our city team did some research and gave me the thumbs up that the funding could go toward neighborhood revitalization, I approached her and said, "How about if we put this toward redevelopment of these historic, inner-city neighborhoods?"

> Yet a Changemaker has the ability to look at things from all different sides, to think outside the box, to take the road less traveled.

Needless to say, she was completely on board, and so were several other commissioners. Yet the one gentleman who had initially proposed putting the surplus toward transit got upset that people didn't want to do what *he* wanted to do. So, he simply refused to vote for it. I had to leave the chambers and go out and beg him to vote for it, because I knew what it would do for the people who lived in those neighborhoods.

Ultimately the strategy worked, and we got the votes we needed. The convention center project could continue, and we were about to begin a critical urban-revitalization project. In fact, this particular revitalization initiative has been the beneficiary of many awards, including the Housing and Urban Development Secretary's Opportunity and Empowerment Award in 2013.

Artists working in all mediums—painters, writers, musicians, sculptors—intuitively use creative solutions to work around problems. They know that no expression of art is perfect. Instead, they constantly adapt and adjust the tone of their instrument, or the colors on their palettes to dial in on the desired result. The same holds true for Changemakers. To solve problems and identify solutions, leaders need to rely on creativity as much as intellect and experience.

> To solve problems and identify solutions, leaders need to rely on creativity as much as intellect and experience.

## The Art of Communication

As an extremely shy kid, it wasn't always easy to communicate. But I firmly believe that my love of reading and writing in part helped me overcome my shyness, because it allowed me to explore new ideas, new concepts, and to open my mind to see new horizons. It begins to build confidence in being open and authentic, two key factors in any Changemaker.

Writing poetry, for example, instills a sense of timing and cadence. You can feel the ebb and flow of a conversation, and you recognize the perfect time to end it or to extend it. This skill holds true not just for communication, but for negotiation as well. So often, when people came before our local government to address an issue, I was able to read that critical point where they had made their case well enough and just needed to sit down and allow for a vote. Unfortunately, though, some people would just go on and on talking, with no sense of timing. And suddenly their moment was gone, and they didn't get their desired outcome.

At the end of the day, artistic expression is about communication. It's a way to convey emotions and opinions, to tell a story, to make others *feel* something. Art has three main purposes: to inform, to educate, and to entertain. To be a Changemaker, you have to harness your inner artist and become a great communicator.

Great works of art invoke emotion and reaction from an audience. That's what I always tried to remember when communicating with my city, and in my post-mayoral days on my radio show. I'll never forget a conversation I had one day with the great jazz trombonist Wycliffe Gordon, a friend who also calls Augusta home. We were discussing how, as a musician, he can feel when he's connecting with his audience. Then he asked me, "Can you feel the connection to your radio audience?" I said, "Absolutely." He smiled and said, "I can, too."

Any musicians or comedians will tell you that they can feel when they're connecting with their audience. That's what a Changemaker has to recognize: in any walk of life, there's always an audience. You are *always* communicating something … both onstage and offstage.

That's a skill set key to being a Changemaker. Having artistic sensibilities allowed me to read my audience and gauge their reaction. If you can't connect with the people you're trying to convince of your point or your platform, then they're not going to get on board. There has to be that connection.

If you can't connect with the people you're trying to convince of your point or your platform, then they're not going to get on board.

## The Art of Performing

Like it or not, leaders are performers. Whether it's a parent or teacher modeling good behavior, an ER doctor or pilot maintaining a calm composure for the sake of those watching them in a time of crisis, a CEO delivering a speech to the senior leadership team, or a senator campaigning, leaders are on stage. Always.

I was speaking to a local civic organization during my first year in office, and a former mayor, a gentleman by the name of Pop Newman, approached me after I spoke and said, "Thank God you've learned the art of brevity." There really is an art to brevity, which is a key component of performing well.

I've sat through probably seventy or more speeches that went on way too long. When I'm on stage, I make sure to focus on my points and remember one rule: always leave the audience wanting more. For me, that comes from learning a sense of timing through a love of words and music.

Performing on stage so often, I was really able to hone my skills with regard to answering questions on the spot quickly and concisely. I never screened any question from any member of any audience I ever spoke to. And having the ability to think on my feet before a live audience helped me tremendously with my communication with the media. They expect you to be able to field all sorts of questions with little to no prep time to get accurate information out to the public.

Changemakers not only need to communicate, they need to perform on the spot ... and *succinctly*. Being able to convey a message or an action plan in time requires the ability to read an audience and stay brief and engaging in such a way that people get it.

## Art Is Subjective

I started recreational writing when I was in the first grade. And I'd always had an affinity for drawing. Around third grade, I began taking art lessons, going from pastels to acrylics over the course of three or four years. I ended up winning several art contests with my paintings, but never really submitted any of my writing in contests. Poetry has always been a passion of mine, and what I do now is write poems for family members and friends. In fact, one year for Christmas, it dawned on me that I could write something for each one of my family members, a gift more personal and special than just buying something that soon may be forgotten.

Over the years, I've seen the impact that poetry can have in people's lives. And it means a great deal to me to know that the pieces I've written for others are framed and still hanging in the houses of loved ones. But what I've found is that, as an artist, when you put your work out there, you also open it up for criticism.

That's one mark of a true artist, and the strength of a Changemaker—knowing you are making yourself vulnerable to criticism, putting yourself out there openly, and welcoming it.

As a leader, your work is going to be criticized. No individual is going to love every piece of art—

> That's one mark of a true artist, and the strength of a Change-maker—knowing you are making yourself vulnerable to criticism, putting yourself out there openly, and welcoming it.

written, painted, or heard—and not everyone you lead will love you. Believe me, not everybody loved me when I was in office. Because if you're making a change, you're making waves, and there is no way to please everyone. But that's alright, you don't need to please everyone. That's just going along with the status quo.

No innovation will ever come from sticking with the status quo. Changemakers are, by definition, innovators, because they think differently; they do things differently.

## Art Is Color-Blind

While I was in office, I had the fortunate opportunity to tour the Charles R. Drew Charter School in the East Lake neighborhood of Atlanta with former Mayor Shirley Franklin. In 1995, the East Lake Foundation was founded to revitalize what was then a struggling inner-city neighborhood. While rebuilding the historic East Lake Golf Club, visionary real estate developer and philanthropist Tom Cousins had a dream of pursuing a holistic approach to revitalization by transforming the surrounding neighborhood into a vibrant community where all residents could thrive. In the beginning, though, friends and colleagues told him he was crazy.

When the school was rebuilt, it became Atlanta's first charter school with a strong focus on arts-based education through the establishment of the Drew Charter School Center for the Arts. Fast forward many years later, and the school has gone from being one of the city's lowest-performing schools to one of its highest. And it remains virtually the same demographic racially. The introduction of the creative arts clearly helped the students to excel in all respects, including academically. The East Lake model for holistic neighborhood revitalization is now being deployed nationally by Purpose

Built Communities with Mayor Franklin serving as executive board chair of the organization.

The bottom line: art assists in community building—it brings people together, it connects and binds us. Government and business can be so institutional, so black and white, cut and dry. Yet art is all colors, not just black or white or red and blue. It doesn't belong to any one culture or any political party. Creative arts contribute to the lives of everyone.

> The bottom line: art assists in community building—it brings people together, it connects and binds us.

## The Power of the Arts

Having been through the municipal-budgeting process here in Augusta on multiple occasions, I've witnessed firsthand the temptation local governments have to cut funding to projects and organizations which contribute to a city's overall quality of life. Oftentimes it seems as though investment in the local arts and culture community rise to the top of the list of potential cuts.

With the primary function of government being to provide basic services to citizens in our communities, this temptation is very easy to understand. However, from an economic-development perspective, quality of life investments are a major factor in business recruitment and something that should never be undervalued.

A real-world example of the importance of local governments having a vested interest in maintaining a focus on their city's quality of life through funding the arts happened while I was mayor in 2012, during our recruitment of a Starbucks manufacturing facility.

Following a long, drawn-out, and very competitive recruitment process, we were made aware that Augusta and one other city had been placed on the company's shortlist. After the announcement finally came that our community would be home to the new facility, with an initial investment of $172 million creating more than 140 new jobs, I had an interesting conversation with one of Starbucks' consultants.

During the course of the conversation, he shared with me that one thing that ultimately helped tip the balance in our favor was the fact that Augusta has a thriving arts and culture community. That was somewhat lacking in the city that was our competitor. He went on to say that incentives do matter, but when a major employer makes a twenty- to thirty-year investment in a community, the quality of life of their employees is a major factor in the decision-making process.

In July of 2012, I had the pleasure of attending the groundbreaking of the new facility, which was covered live by CNN America, *Broadcasting Progress in our Local Economy,* to a worldwide audience. In November of 2017, while heading up the Augusta Economic Development Authority on an interim basis, I also had the pleasure of attending the groundbreaking of a $120 million expansion at the Starbucks plant creating a hundred more new jobs. I believe when you consider that our vibrant arts community contributed heavily to nearly $300 million in investment and the creation of hundreds of new jobs, this makes a strong case that the return on investment our local governments can achieve through investing in the arts is significant. I'm proud to say that our local government here in Augusta continues to invest directly into many arts-based events and initiatives.

While still serving our lead economic-development agency in a consulting role, we hosted two representatives of the Canadian consulate general. The purpose of the visit was to begin a collaboration to explore opening up further business opportunities between Augusta and Georgia's largest trading partner.

Neither of our two guests had visited our community prior to the meeting, and both were amazed to learn of the wide variety of arts and cultural opportunities our city has to offer. I enjoyed sharing with them that the Arts in the Heart of Augusta Festival draws nearly ninety thousand people to our urban core every September to celebrate arts, food, diversity, and culture—with over twenty countries represented in the Global Village.

Although arts and culture are often viewed as niceties in the budgeting process, they can also be *necessities* in helping to seal the deal from an economic-development perspective. These are just two examples of how the strength of our arts and cultural community have served our local economic-development efforts. Though the Starbucks plant is a tangible return on investment, and it remains to be seen where our new relationship with our Canadian friends will lead, in both situations our community's commitment to fostering and enhancing our quality of life simply stood out. Quality of life is hard to define and hard to budget for, but in the end, cities who make it a long-term priority will always be at a competitive advantage for attracting investment.

> Quality of life is hard to define and hard to budget for, but in the end, cities who make it a long-term priority will always be at a competitive advantage for attracting investment.

## The Art of Changemaking

Growing up writing, painting, listening to music, and being in creative environments helped teach me the skill of creative problem-solving, a skill I put to good use every day while spending nine years as a public servant, and I continue to use it to help clients of my business from my current position in the private sector. Where some individuals try to resolve issues with an either/or mentality, it has always been my observation that those leaders exposed to the creative arts have a greater tendency to look at problems from every angle while seeing more than just the monochrome tones of black and white. Where oftentimes the either/or approach can lead to gridlock on an issue, more often than not a creative and multi-faceted approach toward overcoming obstacles results in the same issue simply being resolved.

During my time as mayor of Augusta I relied heavily on my background in the creative arts while viewing the city as a beautiful—yet unfinished—painting on which I could lovingly apply careful brush strokes to help breathe new life into the well-laid foundation established long before my season in office. I also viewed my city as an ongoing narrative in which I could use my leadership role to help author another colorful chapter in its long, rich history.

> I simply applied artistic sensibilities to set a tone to move Augusta forward down a fruitful path, while painting a picture and telling a story of what the future could look like.

In effect, I simply applied artistic sensibilities to set a tone to move Augusta forward down a fruitful path, while painting a picture and telling a story of what the future could look like. Ultimately, this path would lead to the beginnings of transformation for our urban core through major municipal building projects, the revitalization of long-neglected neighborhoods which now engender a sense of civic pride in their residents, and the instilling of a great sense of hope for the future in the citizens I was blessed to serve.

To lead like an artist may not be the first idea that comes to mind when any of us find ourselves inhabiting a leadership role, wherever we may be in our walk of life. However, the ability for leaders to think and act creatively is an attribute of a Changemaker, a skill which when learned will undoubtedly be of lasting benefit to whatever organization you may serve.

With this in mind, I'd like to share five points which should help you think a bit more like an artist in your leadership endeavors:

## 1. Focus on using as many colors on your palate as possible

Great paintings are a beautiful blending of colors that provide contrast and depth while drawing the viewer into them. Rather than relying on any one group or point of view within the organization you serve, make certain to blend these disparate points of view while formulating a path forward. Adding a tone to your canvas you may never have used before will ultimately help paint a much clearer picture of the direction you need to take.

## 2. Focus on being an original

The thing that often sets great works of art apart is simply that they're original. Whether you're developing a city or building a business, you ultimately want to create something that is new and original. Using the building blocks of tried and true principles to establish a foundation is a good way to start, but remember to use that foundation as a platform to go into new directions where others haven't ventured to go. At the end of the day, you simply don't want your work or the narrative around it to look or sound like everyone else's and get lost in the crowd.

## 3. Focus on infusing your work with passion

For me, one of the greatest things about artists is their passion for their work. Instilling this same artistic passion in your leadership role makes your endeavors contagious to those around you. Being extraordinarily passionate about what you do can lead to great heights and depths of feeling, but the end result of passionately pursuing a goal in your leadership efforts will ultimately be of great benefit both to you and to the people around you.

## 4. Focus on creating things that will stand the test of time

When I was in office, I had no authority to issue edicts with regard to how we built new buildings. However, I was able to share my perspective with our city staff that when we built buildings, they should engender a sense of civic pride in our citizens and be structures that, in one hundred years, people would fight to preserve. Whatever work you're focused on creating in your leadership role, keep an eye on the big picture and think how it can be appreciated by future generations and what lessons they can learn from it.

## 5. Focus on instilling as much light into your work as possible

The great Dutch master painters Rembrandt and Vermeer were renowned for their use of light and its ability to draw viewers into the scene before them. Instilling a light at the center of what you're doing as a leader in any position will ultimately achieve the same result by drawing people into your efforts. In leadership roles, whether it be through words or actions, there is always the opportunity to help create a brighter picture of what your efforts are seeking to achieve and how these efforts can contribute to the greater good of the organization you serve.

Great works of art are never created overnight, but rather are brought about by a painstaking attention to detail, a commitment to seeing them through to the end, and an enduring passion toward the creative process. Whether it's in business, government, or any other profession, leading through artistic sensibilities may not seem a common route to choose, but it undoubtedly can lead to the creation of organizations and institutions that will simply stand the test of time while continuing to have a positive impact long after our season of leading them has drawn to a close.

> Great works of art are never created overnight, but rather are brought about by a painstaking attention to detail, a commitment to seeing them through to the end, and an enduring passion toward the creative process.

Whatever leadership role you may find yourself in, stay creative and be a Changemaker!

**TWO CENTS FOR CHANGE**

Taking the road less traveled is not for everyone, and I completely understand this. To choose a different path in life and forge forward can feel like lonely work at times, as its often hard for people, often people you love and respect, to understand why someone would want to put themselves out there in uncharted waters. However, always remember that for transformational change to ever happen there has to be a Changemaker willing to break from the pack and go in a new direction.

1.  In your leadership role, are you leading with passion and from the heart and is your heart truly in it? Whether it's running a business, running a nonprofit, or running for office, to answer this question you need to take a look in the mirror and be honest with yourself.

2.  Are you being creative in your leadership role, or does the product or the vision you're trying to sell look like what everybody else is doing? Remember, innovation comes through doing something differently as opposed to clinging to the status quo. If you're doing something truly new and innovative with faith in the process, you're generally going to be successful.

3.  As a potential Changemaker, are there role models you use in your creative and innovative efforts? Growing up I was a huge Michael Jordan fan—and there were two important lessons I learned from watching him: He always made the team around him better, and if a player or coach talked trash about his team he would go out and hang fifty points

on them the next night. He was truly a Changemaker in sports and a master of creativity whom I've used as a personal role model in my own efforts to create change my entire life.

4.  In your leadership role, have you forgone the spotlight in order to let others around you shine? Being a Change-maker isn't about seeking all the glory, it's about creative problem-solving while, at the same time, inspiring those around you to be better—and creating new Changemakers in the process.

5.  As a potential Changemaker, do you always remember to thank the people around you for their efforts? If you're a Changemaker, you can be the point of the spear, but if people aren't buying what you're selling, you're never going to bring about the desired result of creating positive change in whatever environment you're working in. Never be afraid to give credit where credit's due, and never be afraid to say thank you to the people around you.

chapter four

# Courage: Weather the Storm

*Sometimes flowers grow in the soil of ashes.*
*Pick 'em as you go down Goodbye Road.*

**—JOHNNYSWIM, "GOODBYE ROAD"**

I had been married to my first wife, Kellie, for a few years, but didn't realize the extent of her mental illness. There were times she had psychological breaks and had to be committed for short intervals. It was an incredibly stressful to see and feel her pain and not be able to do anything to help her. And although we had gone through counseling, we eventually got to a point where we mutually decided the best thing would be for us to divorce. We were living in Beaufort, South Carolina at the time, and she desperately needed to go back to Atlanta, to where she felt safe.

Memorial Day weekend, 1997, I was in the midst of purchasing a condominium for her there. Everything finally seemed to be headed in a good trajectory. While in Atlanta, I attended my niece Maggie's graduation as she was named valedictorian of her class at Pace Academy. I'll never forget one of the quotes from her speech about finding the strength to carry on through adversity: "Teddy Roosevelt always said, 'when you come to the end of your rope, tie a knot in it and hang on.'"

On Memorial Day, I returned to Beaufort and that night I got a call from a good friend of ours. Her voice sharp with tension, she told me she couldn't find Kellie. Not long after that, I received a blood-chilling call from the police: Kellie had driven to the parking lot of a church and fatally shot herself. I still have trouble putting into words the overwhelming grief I felt, the confusion, the terrible sadness. I called my father immediately: "Dad, I've made it through a lot, but I just don't know how I can make it through this."

My family rallied around me. I flew to Atlanta, helped make the funeral arrangements, and drove to Kellie's hometown of Columbus, Georgia to bury my wife. So many people attended the service. Friends from New York to South Carolina were there to support me. I remember afterward, night after night, sitting in my house on the stairs and being overcome by guttural sobs of raw pain and emotion. I'll never forget when authorities sent me her pocketbook and I found the receipt for the gun she had used in it. Gut-wrenching and heart-breaking. It took some time, but slowly I healed … by having the support of family, friends, and equally as important, my faith. A tragedy like that oftentimes pushes people to question their faith. Rather than dissipating my faith, however, my wife's suicide made me rely on it more.

But the one person in my life at that time who truly made the biggest difference, who I really owe the world to for her compassion, her understanding, and her friendship, is my current wife, Malisa. She had known Kellie, and we had been friends for years prior. She never pressured me into anything, allowing me the time I needed to heal. Several months went by before we even went on a date. We married in 1999. Life had given me another chance at happiness with a wonderful person who, after over twenty years together, remains my rock and best friend to this day. We've often joked that if she'd known she was going to be married to someone who served in elected office, she may have not signed up for the gig. Her unwavering support has allowed me to undoubtedly say that without her as my partner, none of this would have ever been possible.

> A tragedy like that oftentimes pushes people to question their faith. Rather than dissipating my faith, however, my wife's suicide made me rely on it more.

## Turning a Tragedy into a Message

A Changemaker can get through the most difficult situations and not just survive them but *thrive* beyond them. In the wake of that devastating experience, I found myself equipped and empathetic to people around me who had suicidal thoughts. Through my own personal experience, I've been blessed with the tools and awareness to really help them—and have hopefully helped stop some people from taking that action themselves.

My experiences inspired me to publicly address mental health issues and suicide when I was in office and on my radio show. I made it a point to speak about those critical issues whenever the opportunity arose, and I was given air time, because I know very well they're not easy issues to talk about. But as a Changemaker, you have to be able to open up and talk about your experiences in weathering the storm. I had firsthand knowledge that dealing with mental illness can feel completely isolating for the individual who is suffering with it … and also for the spouse or loved ones. Kellie was estranged from her family and was very guarded about her condition. Apparently, she had been hospitalized several times before we ever met. She had received a slew of diagnoses, from bipolar to schizophrenia. Because I didn't know the extent of it, I never was able to talk to my family during the times that she had mental breaks.

Imagine if somebody falls and breaks a leg but refuses to go to the ER because he or she is too ashamed. That person needs help. With mental illness, something is broken inside—and it's treatable. Just as there isn't any stigma, any shame, or any embarrassment with physical health issues, the same should apply to issues of mental health.

What I learned, and what I went on to share, is that you can't feel ashamed if you or a loved one is dealing with mental health issues. Of course, you always need to respect peoples' privacy, but

> As a Changemaker, you have to be able to open up and talk about your experiences in weathering the storm.

you need your family, your friends, or your counselor. You need to talk to *somebody*. That's one thing that people need to realize: you're never alone. Although it may feel that way when you're going through a tragedy, you're not, so never be afraid to reach out to others and let them support you.

After all, at some point you just might be called on to return the favor.

> That's one thing that people need to realize: you're never alone.

## Lessons in Grief

If there's one concrete, indisputable fact I've learned about life it's that it can, and will, throw you some very wicked curveballs along the way. Whether it's the death of a loved one, the loss of a job, an unforeseen illness, or a major life transition, we're all going to have that moment when life simply rears back and punches you in the mouth.

By the time I was thirty, I had lost my mother to cancer and had become a widower, all within a period of less than four years. Mom was diagnosed with ovarian cancer when I was twenty-four. She had gone through treatment, and we thought that she was doing better. Because she had improved so much, the family was in the midst of planning to get her down to Beaufort, to our family house, for Thanksgiving. Then her health declined.

> If there's one concrete, indisputable fact I've learned about life it's that it can, and will, throw you some very wicked curveballs along the way.

My girlfriend at the time had VIP passes for my birthday to the opening of a Hard Rock Café in Atlanta. But Dad asked me to come home to be with Mom, so I did. I spent my twenty-fifth birthday with her, which in retrospect was incredibly special to have been able to have that time with her. In fact, we were blessed to have the whole family together for Thanksgiving. The morning after, on November 27, just a week after my birthday, she passed. Yet—even though the situation was still very difficult—just having been beside her provided such a strength for all of us.

I was working in banking back in Atlanta at the time, and my job was going well. Then all of a sudden, about six months later, everything caught up with me, crushing my world. The bank where I worked was transitioning through a merger that ended up being very messy, and my job became a terrible environment to go to every day. With the grief of losing Mom still buried inside, one day I simply said to myself: "I've never seen the world. I've been to Europe several times as a kid, but I'm twenty-five years old. If I don't do this now, I'm never gonna do it."

So, I quit my job, hopped a plane, and backpacked around Europe, New Zealand, and Australia. As a child, my parents took the family to Europe where dad's company was headquartered, but they had debated on it, wondering if my sister and I were too young to remember anything. Well, when I went on that backpacking trip, I had the chance to revisit all the places I had gone as a kid with my parents, and I remembered every one of them in such a special way. Deciding to travel for months was cathartic and really cleared my head.

I expected my father to say, "Have you absolutely lost your mind?" But eventually he and my brother John ended up coming to New Zealand and Australia with me for a while, which I think helped with the healing of the three of us. I didn't have a job. I was trying to write the great American novel. I was coaching underprivileged kids in the projects for their afterschool athletics programs. I was just *being*. And I got through that grief and went on to have a successful career in real estate.

One of the things that meant the most to me during this phase of grieving the loss of my mother at a young age was the unwavering support my father gave me. We had always been close, and he had always been the rock of the family. Unfortunately, in 2001 he was diagnosed with Parkinson's disease. A man who was an avid reader, outdoorsman, and golfer, as well as a loving husband, father, grandfather, and friend, spent eight years battling a disease which rendered him unable to pursue his passions any longer. In May of 2009, he finally succumbed to complications from the disease at the age of eighty-four.

In August of that year, Malisa and I went to Bermuda to heal. While we were there, a hurricane began tracking our way, and my executive assistant at the time, Karyn Nixon, kept calling to tell us to get off the island and head back to Augusta. But like my father, the hurricane's name happened to be Bill. I said, "Karyn, I think I'm gonna roll the dice on this one, because I don't think a hurricane named Bill is gonna take me out the year my father passed." Maybe this was faulty logic, but it was also reinforced when Malisa asked a bartender friend of ours named Gilbert if we should leave the island. His answer? "Girlfriend, you'll be fine!" Decision made.

Needless to say, we weathered the storm in Bermuda—both the literal and figurative, actually—and everything turned out fine.

Going through tragedy, literally life and death situations, refines you as a Changemaker. It can help put things in perspective. You gain a sense of compassion. You raise your emotional intelligence and move beyond giving others sympathy to giving them empathy. You understand what the other person is going through. Having gone through so much loss at an early age, the blessing is that it created that empathy in me to where people knew that I understood what they were going through in so many different situations, particularly in dealing with grief and loss.

> Going through tragedy, literally life and death situations, refines you as a Changemaker.

## The Art of Inspiring

If you haven't yet had your breath taken away by the way life can turn on a dime, consider yourself lucky. But also remember that no one makes it through without facing adversity. It's all part of the game, and there isn't anyone or anything that can completely prepare you for it. That's just life.

The key is in what happens after the storm: inspiring others.

Changemakers inherently have a positive bend to their attitudes and a desire to connect with others. And as the last chapter described, there is an art to leadership ... and to Changemaking. The fact is, artists feel deeply. I probably wouldn't have been the kind of mayor I was if I didn't feel as deeply about people as I did. You go through pain. You have to speak at funerals. You lose people you love on a regular basis. But it's that depth of feeling that allows you to connect with the world around you and with individuals to have a positive impact.

As they say, misery loves company, and there's enough personal tragedy out there without dwelling on your own. I don't believe people innately want to be in dark places. That's why it's up to

Changemakers to use any platform they are given to shine a light and create hope to know you don't need to just survive the storm, but you can thrive beyond it.

Too many people get hung up on the question, "Why?" *Why did this happen to me?* I stopped asking "why" a long time ago. A Changemaker accepts that loss and grief and adversity are all part of life. When you put yourself out there and build relationships with people, when you love others, when you invest and care, you will certainly get hurt. But that's *why* I love people. I love getting to know

> That's why it's up to Changemakers to use any platform they are given to shine a light and create hope to know you don't need to just survive the storm, but you can thrive beyond it.

them. I would rather build relationships and risk losing those I love than shut myself out from the world.

Changemakers have to be open, which isn't always easy. When you expose a raw nerve, or you're wounded, there's a natural inclination to shut down. But in order to heal and to cope, you need to be open. To be vulnerable when weathering a tragedy is not the easiest thing, but it's one of the only ways you're gonna get through it. If you don't address the fact that something's broken inside you, it won't heal. Imagine what would happen if you were in a car accident and had internal bleeding. A good doctor knows you can't heal an internal injury from the outside. You need to be opened up.

Being open means seeing the totality of the problem. From an emotional perspective, it means you can't be in a state of denial. In today's world, there's a tendency to think it's easier to sweep things under the rug. But remember that whatever you've swept under it is still going to be there when somebody pulls it up.

---

In today's world, there's a tendency to think it's easier to sweep things under the rug. But remember that whatever you've swept under it is still going to be there when somebody pulls it up.

## The Art of Humor

As I was the mayor of Augusta, the community was watching when I lost my father. As you would expect, condolences came from all over for a man who was a pillar of our community. And I knew, based on my position, that people were watching to see how their mayor handled personal tragedy. I can assure you it's never easy dealing with loss in the public spotlight. I'll never forget a reporter friend asking Karyn if he could interview me prior to the service in the church. Fortunately, Karyn always had my back, and her answer was a resounding "no."

When I spoke at his funeral, I told a story about my father after he was stricken with Parkinson's. He was a man of very few words, and one day I said, "Dad, have you thought about heaven much lately?" He said, "Yep." I said, "Well, Dad, what do you think?" He said, "Sounds like a pretty good deal to me." All business right up until the end.

Despite the somber occasion, the folks in attendance who knew my father well laughed. Appropriate use and timing of humor instantly lightened the mood for those gathered to celebrate his life. And the community saw that a Changemaker's response to dealing with his or her own pain, as well as the pain of others, is to put a smile on peoples' faces, to make them laugh. To bring light into the world in the midst of one's own darkness.

Even in life's most difficult situations, you can still laugh. Sometimes it's about laughing through the tears, but I've found keeping a sense of humor helps you remain full of light within darkness.

> A Changemaker's response to dealing with his or her own pain, as well as the pain of others, is to put a smile on peoples' faces, to make them laugh. To bring light into the world in the midst of one's own darkness.

## The Art of Faith

I've been in banking, I've been in real estate development. I've been in nonprofit work, and I've been mayor. But to me, a job title never defines who you are. That's just a title. While in office, I would tell people, "Being mayor is what I do. My faith is who I am."

Whatever your faith may be, if you don't have strong belief in something, I don't know that you can be a Changemaker. I'm a Christian and I have a strong faith. I don't begrudge anybody else's faith in the least, but if you aren't grounded in some sort of belief and understanding that the work you're doing matters, that you're impacting lives, then I don't believe you can realistically cause positive change.

> While in office, I would tell people, "Being mayor is what I do. My faith is who I am."

To put yourself out there takes faith. And I couldn't have gotten through nine years in office without it.

I still look forward to Augusta Community Prayer Breakfasts every month. Those breakfasts strengthen me and give me hope, because I can physically see a community coming together. It's been going on for thirteen years now, and it's become a source of strength for our city. I think about how many thousands and thousands of people have at least been able to experience it once. Probably thousands more than once, and that to me demonstrates hope. So often we're portrayed as a country or a world divided, but when you get down to the granular level, to the grassroots, you can see that people want to come together, and they want to work together. Through their faith, Changemakers do not divide, they unite.

> Through their faith, Changemakers do not divide, they unite.

My faith teaches me to love my neighbor as myself, and that doesn't come with an asterisk: *Thy rich neighbor, *thy poor neighbor, *thy black neighbor, *thy white neighbor. Neighbor applies to everybody. In my faith, that's not a request … that's a command.

## The Art of Leading through the Storm

Having been through a whole lot of life-changing scenarios along the way, from losing my mother and my first wife prior to hitting the age of thirty, to becoming mayor of the second largest city in Georgia at the age of thirty-eight, there are a few tricks I've learned along the way that can help with making the adjustments and hitting the curves life throws at you.

Here are five ways to help improve your batting average when it happens:

## 1. Always keep your head up

When the inevitable curveball comes, the natural inclination is oftentimes to hang your head and ask yourself "why me?" As easy as it is to want to give up when adversity hits, I can assure you that facing things head on is a much better way to proceed. I've often shared with folks that while storms may rage, the sun is always there above the clouds just waiting to break through. Keep your head up and keep moving forward as there are always brighter days ahead.

## 2. Rely on your teammates

Sometimes when we're going through a rough spot in life, it's easy to simply want to be alone and not be around people. This is definitely understandable and some time to yourself to sort things out is not a bad thing; just make sure not to make it a habit. Whether its family or friends, always remember that you have a team around you who want to help you through whatever difficult situation you may be dealing with, so don't be afraid to lean on them. That's what they're there for, and believe me you'll have multiple opportunities to return the favor as your life progresses.

## 3. Picture yourself as the calm center of the storm around you

I've always been awestruck by the aerial photographs of the centers of hurricanes and how there can be such calm in the midst of so much chaos. It's not easy to do at times, but when the storms of life churn around you, a focus on becoming the calm at the center of it all definitely helps not only you but everyone around you who may be caught up as well. If at times you can't be that calm center, surround yourself with people who help create that sense of calm within you.

## 4. Keep your footing balanced on a strong foundation

It's hard to handle anything in life when you're off balance, and hitting the curves life throws at you is no different. Relying on a strong faith and surrounding yourself with good people are two ways to keep your feet on a foundation that will enable you to weather the storm while keeping your head in the game.

## 5. Keep focused on maintaining your sense of humor

There's an old saying that if you want to make God laugh, tell him your plans. It's a crazy, mixed up world we live in, and there are always going to be things in our lives that don't go according to our plans. Learning to laugh at the absolute absurdity of whatever situation you may find yourself in, as dire as the circumstances may be, helps to put things in perspective. If the laughter is accompanied by more than a few tears that's okay, too. Remember, you're only human, right?

As you deal with the curveballs of life, you're going to strike out every now and again which is perfectly okay. No one is ever going to bat a thousand in this world, and everyone around you has been hit with adversity at some point in their lives. Just always remember to stay in the game and to keep swinging. Before too long you'll be out there teaching others to hit the curves in their own lives as well.

Learning to lead effectively in the face of tragedy is a critical cornerstone of Changemakers from all walks of life. Leaders face both major and minor tragedies in various environments and contexts, whether it's as a corporate leader, a civic or governmental leader, or the leader of a household.

A corporate leader sometimes has to deal with the tragedy of needing to lay people off. Perhaps this isn't a tragedy to the organization overall, but a Changemaker knows it's definitely a tragedy to everybody who gets let go. Displaced workers can't always put food on the family's table, often have to cut back on necessities, and suffer an increase in stress. Good corporate leaders have to make difficult decisions, but they are cognizant of the impact their decisions have on the lives of others on a daily basis.

> Good corporate leaders have to make difficult decisions, but they are cognizant of the impact their decisions have on the lives of others on a daily basis.

The same applies to leaders in the political world. As mayor, I always fundamentally understood that my decisions impacted the lives of everybody I governed … and sometimes not for the better. There were times we had to lay people off in the city, yet as a Changemaker I would make sure to do whatever we could to help them find work. It's in the lesser tragedies where those you lead, as well as those whose lives are impacted, come to understand you have that kind of compassion and realize that you're genuinely trying to do what's right for the majority of the people you serve.

The leader of a household is called upon to be the center of strength during a family tragedy. The month after I left office in January of 2015, Malisa and I mourned the passing of her father, Bruz Boardman. Bruz was, and still is, a local legend in business and was renowned for his larger-than-life personality. Malisa, whom he had spent many years mentoring in order for her to run the family business, was the apple of his eye. He was also like a second father to me and was loved and respected by multiple generations of family and friends. And he was a man who never shied away from doing things differently. Ultimately, he himself was a Changemaker, and though he left a huge void in our family, he went out on his own terms—just the way he lived. Although I realized I could never fill that void for Malisa, I knew it was my time to be there for my wife and to provide as much strength and compassion as I possibly could during her time of grief. Malisa made it through. The business is thriving, and I know that her beloved father, as well as her mother, are proud of the woman she has become.

As Changemakers, we have to be willing to endure the storms. Tragedies are basically inherent in the role of leadership, and unless you're willing to endure those storms, you'll never succeed. You can't be afraid to fail. Weathering a storm is a very tense situation where you can and will get knocked down. You have to be willing to get back up and continue, because weathering a storm takes tremendous patience and persistence.

> Tragedies are basically inherent in the role of leadership, and unless you're willing to endure those storms, you'll never succeed.

The hallmark of a Changemaker is to *always* have that mentality when it comes to the storms in our lives. Change will most certainly come.

## TWO CENTS FOR CHANGE

For my readers in the northern latitudes, you know every single year the mercury is going to drop, and a blizzard is likely to hit. The marrow-tingling, bitter-cold winters are around the corner after the last of the leaves hit the ground. But you also know that spring is going to come one day. The flowers are going to bloom and it's going be hot and you're going to see beautiful skies of blue again. Changemakers see adversity as part of a season.

1.   What have been some of the greatest challenges in your life both professionally and personally and how have you dealt with them? Don't be overly critical on analyzing your performance as you answer this question. Remember, we all become better at dealing with challenges the more we have to face them over time, and patience with yourself and those around you is key to the learning process.

2.   Do you ever recall a situation where you have come to the end of your rope but not given up and looked back on the situation … and been glad you didn't? Overcoming adversity is always difficult, but in the long run it can both lead to personal growth and the opportunity to help others through your own personal experiences.

3.   Do you always try to keep a positive attitude even when things aren't going your way? I can speak from personal experience on this one as, despite being known as a very positive person, like everybody else I've had my own experiences with self-doubt in the face of adversity. However, I've always found my attitude is way easier to control than

the circumstances around me, and in any situation I've faced, it's always helped to keep a good one.

4. Have you ever successfully used humor to lighten the mood in a stressful situation? Believe me, serving in elected office as the point of the spear for a city of 200,000 people was not without its stressful moments. Even so, I always tried to keep the team around me laughing, and we still managed to have some fun and create some great memories that we still talk about today while at the same time successfully getting our jobs done.

5. Have you ever sought help from others on a personal or professional situation you've been dealing with? Asking for help can be difficult for a multitude of reasons. That being said, I firmly believe one of the greatest attributes of a good leader is to seek advice from people who've had more experience dealing with an issue than you have. Whether it's in your personal or professional life, there are mentors out there who want to help you; you just need to find them. In my life, I've been blessed with great mentors who've helped me through difficult times in a variety of situations, both personally and professionally, and I always try to share what they've taught me with others.

# chapter five

# Connecting: Come Together

*It's physically impossible to join hands and work together
if your only focus is pointing fingers and placing blame.*

**—DEKE COPENHAVER**

If you want to know the pulse of the community you live in, there's no better place than the steam room at the local YMCA. Because when you're sitting in a steam room with a bunch of sweaty dudes after a workout, trust me, everyone is on an equal level. And no matter who you may be, everyone is perfectly comfortable in shooting each other straight. No airs. No pretenses. Just straightforward conversations on multiple topics which, more often than not, include politics. When I first took office, I was committed to staying in touch with the people I served. I wasn't going to stop shopping at Lowe's on the weekend or stop visiting the YMCA every morning.

That sense of connection I learned from my father. He always took time to walk the floor of the plant where he served as CEO, because he never saw himself above the people he worked with. Or those who worked for him. In a leadership position, placing yourself on a pedestal or in an ivory tower isolates you from the people you're serving and serving with.

> **Changemakers never consider themselves to be above those they serve.**

Changemakers never consider themselves to be above those they serve. That's the only way to get the community to come together.

## Change Can't Happen in a Vacuum

My life intersects with many people from many walks of life, but a lot of folks get stuck in their silos. Being mayor took me far out of my comfort zone. So far, in fact, that it actually *became* my comfort zone. I got so used to being in diverse groups and listening to opposing viewpoints that I just don't think I could go back to only hanging around in one silo.

I find that meeting new people and really understanding what makes them tick to be one of the most exciting and interesting parts of life.. I'll talk about the important issues that really move folks: faith, leadership, family, politics. What I've found, as I've said before, is that we're really not so different after all. And I've found most people have some conservative views and some liberal views as well. Opinions and viewpoints can change over time, and that's okay. Changemakers are always open to learn, especially from others. How can you possibly grow as a person if you only hang around people who look like you and think like you? Changemakers seek the humanity in people. And that's critical in bringing people together, because at the end of the day, people want to be included and to know they matter.

> Changemakers are always open to learn, especially from others. How can you possibly grow as a person if you only hang around people who look like you and think like you?

Somebody once asked me on my radio show, "If Augusta was a food, what would it be?" I said, "It would be a gumbo. And we all know that gumbo wouldn't be any good if it only had one ingredient."

## The Art of Inclusion

Augusta's race for mayor in May 2018 resulted in a 26 percent turnout. I remember somebody saying, "Well, that was a better turnout than some cities in the state." I was appalled. How can you be excited when 74 percent of your citizens who are registered to vote don't even bother to show up?

Clearly, it's not going to be politics that brings energy and enthusiasm to the community, but the kind of positive and impactful change only driven by the private sector. So, when Augusta's convention and visitors bureau put together a master plan called Destination Blueprint and asked me to get involved in 2018, I couldn't wait to roll up my sleeves. The in-progress plan has three prongs: telling Augusta's story both internally and externally, enhancing the downtown, and creating new attractions. I felt like this was exactly the kind of growth in the economy, the kind of opportunity and excitement, that Augusta needed to coalesce the community around. People would come together around the campaign, and that physical manifestation of people working together and excited about improving their city would spark a movement.

Campaigns are not for everybody, either by design or by default. But I wanted this to be something that any citizen in our community could join to really transform the city, to shape its future. So, I enlisted many younger leaders in the community, including Barclay Bishop. She's a very sharp local anchor who hosts the morning show on our ABC affiliate and someone I've been friends with for years. Because the campaign has a five-year timeframe, she was provided the unique opportunity to be included by being able to make a significant monetary pledge over five years. "I thought to be a part of a campaign like this, you would have to write the check for $100,000 and up," she said. "But to know that my pledge gives me an equal seat at the table is an experience I never thought I'd have."

## Inspiring People to Follow Instead of Forcing Them

I've always found that if you are willing to work with everybody, everybody is usually willing to work with you. That establishes trust. And to instill a sense of trust in people helps them to be inspired to work with you. I never asked anybody to do something that I wouldn't do myself.

In 2009, our community began hosting the IRONMAN Augusta 70.3, which is North America's largest half IRONMAN race. The event begins with a 1.2-mile swim, followed by a 56-mile bike ride, and finishes up with a 13.1-mile run. I've been fortunate to complete the event five times, and part of the reason I began doing it in the first place was to inspire the community to get healthier. I didn't participate the first year, but being competitive, I shared from the stage as I thanked the athletes for coming: "Y'all are making me feel lazy ... so next year I'm in." I figured if I said that publicly, I couldn't back out. And that's how I ended up becoming a triathlete.

Despite the fact that the race is considered an individual sport, I've often shared with people that to my mind, being out on a course with fifteen hundred athletes cheering each other on with a whole lot of crowd love on the run course is truly the biggest team experience I've had in any sport I've ever participated in. The professionals in the event are amazing athletes, but the most inspiring thing to me is the people, many with disabilities and cancer survivors, who simply gut it out just to finish the race. The event has always underscored for me the power of community and the energy around people coming together in the pursuit of a common goal.

My most memorable race was back in 2013. I had trained hard that year with the goal of setting my personal record. Through doing the event several years prior, I had developed a great friendship with an amazing young lady named Brittany Banker. Brittany is a single mother, a two-time cancer survivor, and a tremendous athlete who has completed multiple half and full IRONMAN competitions. The week prior to the race, Brittany (who wasn't competing that year) and I had lunch, and I shared my goal with her.

During the race the following Sunday, I ended up tweaking my calf at mile five of the run and had to gut it out with a limp for the last eight miles. When I was nearing the finish, the pain was so bad that I was walking. Then Brittany burst out of the crowd and told me I needed to run it out to set my personal record. I told her about my calf, but she wasn't having any of it. I began to run again with Brittany running alongside me before she rejoined the crowd at the finish line. With the finish line in sight, I began to sprint it out and finished the race in six hours, sixteen minutes, and fifty-six seconds, setting a new personal record. I then proceeded to throw up in a trash can, which was caught on tape by our local NBC affiliate who interviewed me immediately thereafter. Through Brittany's inspiration, I had given it my all, and I definitely left everything on the course that day!

Changemakers know they are always setting an example and always recognize the opportunity to inspire. I'd even ignite that spark of inspiration in young people, telling them, "You're never too young to volunteer. And you're never too young to be a leader. If you see trash in your neighborhood, go pick it up. Or get your friends and work together. Because when people see you doing it, it's more than likely they're gonna do it as well."

> Changemakers know they are always setting an example and always recognize the opportunity to inspire.

That's the only real power that should matter to leaders and to Changemakers: the power to inspire. If you're using control and manipulation to get your desired outcome, that is not changemaking. That's bullying.

As General Patton said: "A piece of spaghetti or a military unit can only be led from the front end."

## The Inspiration of the Godfather of Soul

On April 18, 2006, in my first year in office, I met James Brown, the Godfather of Soul, when he served as the honorary starter for the Tour De Georgia leg that opened in Augusta. His first words to me were that he "knew my people" and that I was so "new and now" and that "this town ain't never gonna hold ya'!"

As a lifelong fan, I was just blown away by his aura, his knowledge, and his passion for his hometown—a place that hadn't always given him his rightful due. The man simply personified what it meant to be cool. We immediately struck up a kinship through a mutual love for music and a shared love of Augusta. From that moment forward, I took every opportunity I had to thank him for his contributions to the city. And he took every opportunity to show his love for Augusta to a worldwide audience, while at the same time revolutionizing the world of music and establishing a legacy that lives on to this very day.

My first memory of Mr. Brown following our meeting was when I received a package in the mail from him, all the way from Ireland where he was on tour. It was a small clock with a golfer on it, the inscription read: "Longest Drive." I was just blown away by the idea that he had taken the time to give me a second thought on one of his many world tours. Needless to say, I treasure that clock!

The next time I recall hearing from him was in the early fall of that same year, when I was given a message to call him. Once again, I was astounded that the Godfather of Soul was reaching out to me. As I called him on my cell on the way home from work, I remember the conversation vividly as we discussed music, religion, and politics … basically all the topics that polite southerners were taught to steer clear of in social conversation. At one point Mr. Brown stopped and said, "Man, Deke, you're just like a Kennedy! Black people love you!"

Coming from someone who had been an integral part of those tumultuous times in the sixties—having even helped to quell a potential riot through his concert in Boston on April 5, 1968 in the wake of Dr. King's assassination the day before—these words truly meant something. No cooler words have ever been spoken to me before or since.

On October 15, 2006, we were side by side for the dedication of the James Brown Arena, as our local civic center was renamed in his honor. I'll never forget that he asked me to speak first on the program. Having run to fulfill an unexpired term the prior year, I was running for a full term that year, and the honor Mr. Brown bestowed upon me came during the midst of my second mayoral campaign. The prior year, the point had been made that I had "crossed over" in the mayor's race, as races here had historically gone more or less along racial lines. After I had spoken, Mr. Brown took the time to share with the crowd his support for me and his heartfelt feelings on the job I was doing as mayor.

Leading up to that point, I had many members of the African-American community share quietly with me that they had supported me and would again in that election. However, after the Godfather did what he did in his own special way, I'll never forget how that support turned vocal with people throughout the crowd coming up to me after the ceremony letting me know that they wanted yard signs as soon as possible. A seminal moment in my life was simply made possible by the love and support of my friend Mr. James Brown.

A seminal moment in my life was simply made possible by the love and support of my friend Mr. James Brown.

Following a strong victory that November, I had two more meetings with the Godfather of Soul in early December of 2006. One where we were guests on a local cable-access show, and he brought his newly minted UK Music Hall of Fame Award, which awed me to hold it in my hand. The next was at his final James Brown Christmas Toy Giveaway where we, along with his family and friends, distributed toys to children the Thursday before his passing on Christmas morning. I'll never forget our final on-camera interview and him telling me before we went on that he had chills on what to me was one of those muggy, rainy days that you can only get in winters in the south.

That Monday Christmas morning, the phone rang at my father-in-law's house where my wife and I had spent the night for Christmas Eve. It was a local TV station calling to request an interview ... and to let me know that Mr. Brown had passed. We were having the whole family over to our house for Christmas that day and had set a policy of not doing interviews from the house. For my friend Mr. Brown, however, I broke my policy that morning. I'll never forget doing that interview in our den in front of the fireplace and sharing with the reporter that now, in the wake of his passing, local citizens would have the opportunity to see what this man meant to the world. Later in the day I had my nephew William sit in while I did a live telephone interview with the BBC from my home office.

In the days leading up to his homegoing service, at the arena now named in his honor, our city team planned furiously for an event that would be befitting of the Hardest Working Man in Show Business, knowing that the world would be watching. On that Saturday, a capacity crowd gathered in unity for a four-hour service to say good-bye to a musical icon and a man who was dedicated to helping his community. Among those in attendance were Jesse

Jackson, Al Sharpton, MC Hammer, Michael Jackson, and Chuck D. from Public Enemy. The family invited me out to pray before they brought his casket in. As I stood there in a prayer circle with Jesse Jackson, Al Sharpton, and the family, two thoughts hit me: "I'm standing in the midst of a historic moment," and "How in the world did I end up becoming a part of this?" Opening yourself up and putting yourself out there can definitely lead to creating both moving and memorable moments in life.

Jesse Jackson recognized me from the stage. He said, "Mr. Mayor, I wanna thank you for being here and for staying," because Malisa and I stayed for the entire service. I didn't think that was anything out of the ordinary. That's what you do to show your respect for a friend, and for someone who meant so much to the world.

For many of those hours, the world watched as CNN went live to televise the service attended by politicians, musicians, comedians, and just your average man and woman on the street who wanted to pay their respects. I remember thinking how proud I was of our city for giving this great man the respect that he so richly deserved. I knew Mr. Brown was smiling down from heaven.

In the end, I will always carry a feeling of gratitude and love in my heart for a man I had always admired, and whose friendship I truly valued. I also came to understand fully in that wonderful season of my life what it meant to have the blessing of the Godfather, and the epitome of a Changemaker dedicated to inspiring others.

# Don't Judge a Book by the Red Leather Cover

To bring people together, a Changemaker knows not to judge people before he or she gets to know them, to always keep an open mind and an open heart. People are incredibly complex, and if you let them, they will amaze you. But too many times it seems like there's a natural tendency to want to paint groups of people with a broad brush.

Would you be shocked to know that James Brown was a Republican? That's right: the Godfather of Soul was a conservative Republican who actually endorsed Richard Nixon for president. I once had the Reverend Al Sharpton and Deanna, James Brown's daughter, on my radio show. At one point, Reverend Sharpton said, "Mr. Brown was a

> To bring people together, a Changemaker knows not to judge people before he or she gets to know them, to always keep an open mind and an open heart.

conservative Republican, and we rarely ever agreed politically. But he was like a father to me. And you know, Deanna, if Mr. Brown was here, he'd say, 'Rev., y'all need to respect Mr. Trump.'"

Reverend Sharpton is truly a funny guy with a wonderful sense of humor. I don't know if everybody in America would think of Al Sharpton that way, but he is. I might not always agree with his politics, but that doesn't mean I can't appreciate his sense of humor. It's sad to think we get these personas in our heads, likely influenced by the media, that make us think a person is one way when he or she is really another. Unfortunately, public figures often become

> I've never met a public figure who didn't have a very real, very human side. I've always found that seeking to know this side of anyone you meet makes it much easier to bring people together on common ground.

caricatures of themselves in people's minds based on the way the press portrays them, but I've never met a public figure who didn't have a very real, very human side. I've always found that seeking to know this side of anyone you meet makes it much easier to bring people together on common ground.

That's what I love about James Brown—his music brought people together. And as huge a star as he was, he was *present*. It wasn't unusual to see him at a grocery store or at a local bar downtown. And not just in Augusta, but the world loved him in that red, leather jumpsuit—different races, different socioeconomic backgrounds, different cultures, different generations.

When I first ran for mayor, and for nine years in office, one of my primary focuses was to heal the racial divide here in Augusta. It has always been my firm belief that a house divided against itself will never stand. And in spite of our differences, citizens in local communities everywhere should never take an "us and them" attitude toward the places they choose to call home. At the end of the day, it's ultimately all "us."

> The street that runs in front of my front door is connected to yours. The wind doesn't stop blowing nor the river flowing along any perceived political, racial, or socioeconomic lines.

Loving our neighbors as ourselves has nothing to do with categorizing people as our black neighbors, our white neighbors, our rich neighbors, our poor neighbors, or placing labels on any other group who we think fits within the context of what our neighbors should or shouldn't look like. In the end, people from all walks of life who live in communities are all neighbors in my book. The street that runs in front of my front door is connected to yours. The wind doesn't stop blowing nor the river flowing along any perceived political, racial, or socioeconomic lines.

To put into context my views on race prior to taking office, I'll share with you a very personal story: I grew up in the south, and hearing racial epithets used on a regular basis was something that was commonplace. It never truly registered on me, it was just the world I lived in. That all changed for me in the early nineties when I was living in Atlanta and working for what was then Nations Bank, what is now Bank of America. During that time, my best friend at the office was a true gentleman by the name of Mark Jones, who happened to be African American. I say "happened to be" because it didn't really matter to me what the color of his skin was, he was simply just a very cool, very intelligent, very laid-back cat who was a real pleasure to be around. The kind of guy I couldn't imagine anyone *not* wanting to hang out with.

Ultimately Mark and I, as sales assistants for the securities division, had the opportunity to spend a week together in a hotel to join in a cram course to get our Series 7 securities license. After dinner one night, following an extremely exhausting day of learning the intricacies of financial transactions, Mark made a statement that would change my life forever. He said, "You know what? If my skin color was yours, we'd be the same people. And if your skin color was mine, it would be the same way."

At that seminal moment in my life, I came to the realization that any racial epithet I heard from that point forward was not only directed at any given race but was also directed at my friend Mark. To this very day and I am truly grateful for my friendship with Mark, and for the impact his words had on my life.

Years later when I ran for mayor in 2005, I was extraordinarily blessed to have been invited to speak at a multitude of African-American churches. I always realized the poetic irony in this—having grown up a shy kid from Canada, I always felt more at ease in those situations than I ever did at any club I had ever been a member of. On my thirty-eighth birthday, I had the opportunity to spend six hours in two different church services where I once again found a tremendous appreciation for being welcomed in, warts and all, to a congregation that truly got what it meant to be a part of something larger than yourself and to be a part of a community. I'll never forget standing before the congregations of Macedonia Baptist Church and Beulah Grove Baptist, sharing with them my unwavering opinion that I would be more pleased to see 100 percent turnout at the voting booth than to be elected and realizing what impact the fact that I was totally sincere had on their church families.

Having been invited to attend services at so many African-American churches during my campaign, I repeatedly heard from the people I met that politicians came around during election season and then didn't return until the next campaign. I was actually shocked to hear this, as I couldn't imagine people buying a candidate's care and concern if that person only did "drive-bys" during an election. With this in mind, Malisa and I continued to attend services at different churches throughout my time in office. We also made it a point of moving the Mayor's Prayer Breakfast to churches and places of worship throughout the community. As I mentioned earlier, one trait of a Changemaker is to have a sustained presence with the people you serve. With Martin Luther King Jr. as one of my personal heroes, I made it a point to attend every service held on King Day, which ended up making it my busiest day of the year with services and events beginning early in the morning and running until late in the evening. For me, working to heal the racial divide meant showing a sustained commitment toward getting to know and establish relationships with people throughout the community of all different ethnicities. Basically, I knew I had to walk it like I talked it, and a drive-by during election season just wasn't going to cut it.

In the end, I was blessed to have been elected by a large majority three times in a predominantly African-American southern city. I firmly believe that I was blessed to have this opportunity through being sincere, speaking from the heart, and spending quality time in all parts of the community I was honored to serve. I also fully believe that the issues created in other cities (although Augusta continues to have its own issues to deal with) are fostered by sections of communities oftentimes being pitted against each other while having no meaningful interaction with each other. Where there isn't interaction, a sense of mistrust begins to build, which can often create a powder keg that's just waiting to ignite.

> I knew I had to walk it like I talked it, and a drive-by during election season just wasn't going to cut it.

The more leaders can bring together people of all walks of life and differing backgrounds on common ground the better, as I've witnessed firsthand that constant interaction builds bridges of trust while replacing the walls built by mistrust. I also found during my time in office that oftentimes, in order to find common ground, you must *become* the common ground. And to do this as a Changemaker, people have to trust you and your motives.

> In order to find common ground, you must *become* the common ground.

Ultimately the Changemaker's choice is: do we build walls or build bridges?

# A Southern Gentleman … from Canada

One fond memory I have during my time in office was when we had our annual St. Patrick's Day parade. There was a viewing stage, and mayoral protocol meant that I was to sit on it. I looked out in the crowd and saw Betty Beard, one of our city commissioners, who was actually mayor pro tempore and happens to be African American. Betty and I had established a good working relationship, and it was her, in fact, who ended up casting the deciding vote for the Laney Walker/Bethlehem Revitalization Project. She didn't have a seat on the stage, so I went down into the crowd and brought her up to the stage and gave her mine.

I didn't do it to accomplish a goal. I did it because it was the right thing to do. But I have to think that showing somebody kindness and respect builds trust, and that one act may have helped transform a neighborhood by breathing new life into it through a long-term and ongoing revitalization initiative, bringing new construction and hundreds of new residents into a place which once was the epicenter of Augusta's urban blight.

# The Art of Consensus-Building

Despite our socioeconomic, racial, ethnic, gender, or faith-based differences, we're all human beings who are trying to meet our basic needs on a daily basis. I would submit that this simple underlying fact contributes to the common ground being fertile ground, where great ideas and great initiatives can flourish … while the extremes of any entity or organization are imbued with rocky soil, which makes it difficult, if not impossible, to plant a healthy crop.

Heartfelt consensus-building in businesses, communities, or any organization is a powerful tool for impacting employees, citizens, or anyone else participating in the process, as it gives them a voice and brings them together around a common cause.

Although this isn't an exhaustive list, here are five ways to get started in the process:

## 1. Check your preconceived notions at the door

We're all socialized in a multitude of different circumstances based on the environments in which we're raised. Just because someone looks different, acts different, or thinks different from us, it doesn't make them the enemy or our polar opposites as human beings. I've actually found just the opposite in that people I wouldn't seem to have anything in common with, from many different backgrounds, different parts of the world, and different walks of life, share my common interests and values. Whether it be a love of family and friends, an appreciation of their heritage, an appreciation for music, an interest in sports, or just the enjoyment of a good laugh, I've usually found in meeting new people that you probably have more in common than you think, and you can usually find something to bond over.

## 2. Be sincere

A word to the wise, if your heart is not into the endeavor of consensus-building and you can't sincerely express why you've got it as a goal in any platform you're trying to address it from, don't try it in the first place, as your efforts won't be well received. No focus group or well-paid moderator can ever accomplish the goal of building consensus like someone who speaks from the heart can. If you can't speak with sincerity, this type of effort just won't work and will ultimately cause more problems than solutions.

### 3. Show trust to receive trust

One of the biggest impediments to building consensus is formed around a simple lack of trust among all involved. Trust is a funny thing in that it usually has to be earned before it's ever given. Although it may be counterintuitive to most people, the best way to earn trust is to ultimately go completely against the grain and to trust people until they might give you a reason not to. If you get burned, you get burned. But completely opening yourself up to a group with trust and never expecting it to be reciprocated will ultimately bring more trust back your way than you would ever imagine. Trust me on that one!

### 4. Be honest about your fear and get out of your comfort zone

Let's be honest, there are times when we live in an overly homogenous society where like associates with like, and we can be a tad bit afraid of associating with people who aren't in our comfort zone. Don't deny this fact when undertaking a true effort to build consensus, just own up to it—and the quicker you do the faster it goes away. I've always found myself way, way out of my comfort zone more times than I'd like to admit. And the number-one way to make that go away is admitting it and laughing about it. Believe me, when people say laughter is the best cure, it definitely is as I've laughed myself through a tremendous amount of uncomfortable situations in life. Admitting your fear, moving outside your comfort zone, and laughing at the awkwardness of any situation goes a long way toward establishing bonds and building consensus.

## 5. Don't be afraid to fail!

Let's face it, in a world of reality TV shows and hyperpartisan politics, things like civility, sportsmanship, and consensus-building might not get the headlines. Sometimes people who focus on these things might fail in their efforts to win an election or a big pay raise. If your efforts to build consensus don't succeed at first, don't feel like you've failed. Just taking that first step toward bringing people together around a common cause is a win in and of itself.

## The Art of Unity

I must admit, it's increasingly disappointing to me to see how divided our nation appears to be politically. When I think back to 9/11, as tragic as the events of that day were, they ultimately served as an example of the strength of our nation's resolve and bound us all together through a shared compassion for our fellow citizens, whose lives would never be the same after that day.

Although it came about through tragedy, in the weeks and months following those heinous acts, there seemed to be a sense that we were all Americans first as opposed to being a nation defined by our political affiliations. Unfortunately, today it seems as though political campaigns are built around demeaning, dehumanizing, and demonizing the opponent due in large part to their party affiliation. However, in spite of the uninspiring, vitriolic, and hyperpartisan nature of today's political landscape, I believe that, beneath the surface, our nation is not as divided as some may think.

I was once asked to speak to a local Sunday school about my perspective on our community and how the church, St. Augustine of Canterbury Episcopal, could make a greater impact through their outreach efforts. In setting the tone for the morning, I shared with those gathered that to some, our community seemed to be divided based on local politics, but that I saw a different picture. I went on to point out that in my morning workouts at the family YMCA, I had long ago noted that my fellow members comprise a true cross section of our community based upon a diversity of ages, ethnicities, faiths, socioeconomic status, political affiliations, and genders. I then made the point that it reminded me of a family, in that if you were absent for any length of time, people actually missed you and inquired where you had been upon your return. Using this as an example, I shared with those gathered that the people I see at the YMCA each morning represent what Augusta looks like to me, which seems to be more united and less divided.

In further painting a picture of the beautifully diverse tapestry of our community, I then referenced our Annual Arts in the Heart of Augusta Festival. In 2018, the event drew over eighty-eight thousand people to downtown Augusta to celebrate food, arts, diversity, and culture. With more than twenty countries represented, the festival has become a "not-to-miss event" for locals and visitors alike, taking place without incident for thirty-seven years now. I made the point

> In spite of the uninspiring, vitriolic, and hyperpartisan nature of today's political landscape, I believe that, beneath the surface, our nation is not as divided as some may think.

that any community that hosts an event of this magnitude each and every year would not appear to me to be a divided community, but rather a community where diversity is not only recognized but celebrated. Once again, I shared that Arts in the Heart represents for me the face of Augusta.

Finally, to underscore the strength of our community, I told the story of what I saw in 2014 during our historic local ice storm. In all my years as mayor, I felt as though this was Augusta's finest hour, as local governments and local citizens worked together seamlessly to help those individuals and families whose lives had been impacted by the catastrophic storm. I went on to share with those gathered that the message to come together as a community to help our friends and neighbors during their hour of need didn't have to be spoken—as our local citizens simply knew it was the right thing to do. Once again, what I saw was a community united as opposed to a community divided.

I closed by pointing out that Augusta is by no means a perfect community, and that there are issues to be resolved, chief among them our high poverty rate and a need for continuing to improve the educational outcomes of our local youth. I suggested that their church, as home to many retired educators, would be a welcomed mentoring and tutoring partner in a local school. I also shared my perspective that there can be no "community" without "unity" and that unity in any community has to come from the grassroots up by efforts like theirs as opposed to from the top down.

Many years after 9/11, I still believe in the strength of our nation and the yearning of most of America's citizens to find causes to rally around as opposed to perpetually being led to focus on issues which divide us. I also firmly believe that local governments can, and should, play a major role in moving our nation beyond the hyperpartisan political quagmire we now find ourselves in by setting the example of what true commitment to putting public service above party politics can look like.

And as Changemakers, it's our job to get the community to come together, for as our communities rise or fall, we all rise or fall.

> And as Changemakers, it's our job to get the community to come together, for as our communities rise or fall, we all rise or fall.

**TWO CENTS FOR CHANGE**

In a world often seemingly hell-bent on embracing extremism, finding common ground might seem like it's an almost impossible thing to do. But in reality, it's not.

At the grassroots level, there are good people who want to find it, and who are tired of being played off of each other by individuals, institutions, and organizations that don't seem to have their best interests, much less their common interests, in mind. I've witnessed firsthand the true power of consensus-building through seeking common ground with a passion and the transformational impact it can have on communities and the lives of the citizens who call them home.

1.  In your personal or professional life, have you ever felt like you were caught up in something bigger than yourself, where you put others needs before your own? I'll never forget my first run for office when a ragtag group of twenty- and thirtysomethings who knew nothing about how to run a campaign propelled me to victory. When I made my announcement, it was brutally hot, and my friend Scott Davis, while handing out water, came up with our campaign slogan—"A Refreshing Change"—on the spot. It was at that moment I realized we were all involved in something that was bigger than any one individual.

2.  Have you ever had a preconceived notion about an individual or organization proven to be off base when you got to know more about them? As I mentioned in this chapter, I doubt most people would think James Brown's political views were conservative, but in the end his connection

with the world had little to do with his politics and everything to do with the funky beat in music the Godfather of Soul pioneered.

3. Personally or professionally, have you ever let a fear of failure stop you from pursuing an endeavor you are passionate about? Let's be honest, we all have a fear of failure and I've dealt with it like everybody else. But in the end, I've come to realize that in life you learn more from your failures than you do from your successes. Ultimately, true success is born out of a whole lot of failed attempts.

4. Have you ever taken time to consider how someone with an opposing view to your own on a topic might have developed that viewpoint? Any successful organization is comprised of a team of people who have opposing viewpoints but are able to work together toward a common goal. As a changemaker, you have to be able to listen without prejudice to all points of view and figure out how they can fit within the framework of your team goal.

5. Have you ever purposely focused on using consensus-building to solve a problem? I'll be the first to admit that in a "we-want-it-now" world, consensus-building leadership in any organization is difficult, and it takes a tremendous amount of time and energy. When I did my first half IRONMAN, Grace Forgay, the daughter of some great friends of ours, gave me a plaque that reads: "There are no shortcuts to anyplace worth going." There are no shortcuts to working to build consensus to resolve issues, but in the end this method of problem-solving is definitely someplace worth going.

# Listening:
# Learn from Others

*Wisdom is the reward you get for a lifetime of*
*listening when you'd have preferred to talk.*

**—DOUG LARSON**

A young man who works at my local YMCA and I are both huge
college football fans. But with me being a Georgia fan and him being
an LSU fan, he didn't just like to talk about football—he liked to talk
trash. He's a good bit younger than me, and one day something just
hit me when he was trash-talking about the upcoming football game.

Finally, I said, "Chris, I just realized that the good Lord gave us all two eyes, two ears, and one mouth for a reason. That tells me that we should spend two thirds of the time watching and listening and one third of the time talking. You might want to consider that."

Chris and I are still friends, but he doesn't talk trash the way he used to.

I learned the art of listening from my father. I remember when I was asked to sit on various boards of directors, his advice to me was priceless: "One thing you need to remember is don't speak just to hear yourself talk. If you have something to add to the conversation, then by all means say it, if it helps the situation. But don't feel like you ever *need* to speak. Sometimes silence is better than speaking."

> Don't feel like you ever *need* to speak. Sometimes silence is better than speaking.

So often I drew from this in office. When I would receive calls from people who had an issue, or from those who were upset, I learned that if I simply listened and didn't try to interject myself into the issue unnecessarily, most people would talk themselves through their own problems. I realized most people just want somebody to listen to them.

I think it's a natural reaction to want to fill in the silence. It can be extremely uncomfortable to sit there, saying nothing. But in order to really hear people out, sometimes we need to be comfortable in our own silence. I learned that lesson early in my second marriage. Malisa and I were discussing something, and without jumping to generalities, raised as a guy in this society, I tended to want to fix things. She said, "Look, I don't need you to fix my problems. I want you to just listen to me." And that for me, coming from my wife, was a great and powerful lesson.

Listening establishes trust. And if you're able to make people feel comfortable enough to start talking and communicating, you establish a trust and a connection worthy of a Changemaker.

## A Mile in Their Boots

I've found that when considering the art of communication, it's always good to remember that it's hard for people to get your message if they feel like you're ignoring theirs.

Everyone wants to feel heard. Everyone wants to feel connected. Everyone wants to feel appreciated and especially respected, even if you don't agree with their opinions. Only then can you truly have a conversation and resolve problems. Part of the problem, however, is that we live in a vastly impatient society, and it takes patience to listen. Fear plays a role as well. It's hard to hear what others have to say sometimes. There's a tendency to want to influence them before they get a chance to speak.

> Everyone wants to feel heard. Everyone wants to feel connected. Everyone wants to feel appreciated and especially respected, even if you don't agree with their opinions.

But it's in that ability to listen where change can happen.

Before they can inspire, Changemakers need to connect. There's no other way around it. And if a leader can't establish that emotional connection with people, he or she will never inspire them to do anything.

Changemakers make people feel valued, protected, and that their voices are being heard. You can get results if you are willing to be a tyrant and not have that personal connection. You can certainly use fear and manipulation to get your desired outcome. But in the process you end up building enemies. And ultimately, those you serve will want to see you fail.

Changemakers are willing to put themselves in another's shoes. Throughout my life, I've tried to make it a point to spend time in lots of other environments—impoverished neighborhoods, with other ethnicities and cultures, at different churches.

In fact, at Fort Gordon there's a great program called Augusta in Army Boots, designed to give folks a real world sample of what it's like to be in the military. You spend two days and a night at the fort, and they outfit you with your uniform. You go out on the firing range. You even get to do late-night maneuvers and engage in a simulated firefight.

I've always had a strong connection with the military, so I volunteered to put myself in their boots. I thought, I was just going to take orders, but I ended up volunteering to be the platoon commander with fifteen people under me.

If I had tremendous respect for the military prior to that experience, it jumped up exponentially afterwards. After a day and a half of a lack of comfort, a lack of sleep, and some pretty frightening, unknown situations, I could only imagine what it would be like to be deployed for months or years at a time. Subject to *live* fire, not just a simulation. It just gave me such an appreciation, such empathy for our brave men and women in uniform.

Following that experience, whenever someone would say that I had a tough job as mayor, I'd reply, "Being mayor of a city of 200,000 people is not easy. But

> **It is critical that Changemakers walk in another's shoes, that they get a taste of what another's life is like.**

after spending time with my friends at Fort Gordon, at least I'm not being deployed for six months at a time. Or having to leave my family. Or being shot at constantly."

It is critical that Changemakers walk in another's shoes, that they get a taste of what another's life is like.

## Not Being Heard: A Millennial Outcry

Part of adjusting to change for leaders means coming to grips with the reality that we must pass the baton of leadership willingly, as opposed to holding onto it with a clinched fist. In order for our cities and our businesses to be sustainable, new leadership over time isn't just a nicety, it's a necessity. Having the ability to recruit and retain the best and brightest young minds possible is ultimately the lifeblood of any organization. To keep this lifeblood flowing, the next generation of leaders, of Changemakers, must not simply be analyzed and categorized, they must be engaged.

I've often found myself in board meetings or on task forces where one particular question seems to come up again and again: how do we engage millennials? Ironically, nine times out of ten there's no one under the age of forty sitting in the room. In speaking to my younger friends about this situation, there seems to be a consensus that their voices aren't being heard, because they're generally

> In speaking to my younger friends about this situation, there seems to be a consensus that their voices aren't being heard, because they're generally not included in these discussions, and if they are, they're talked over and not with.

not included in these discussions, and if they are, they're talked over and not with.

Growing up and during my young adult life, I was blessed to have many mentors, with my father chief among them. I remember being taught life lessons by men and women who shared them willingly, which has benefited me in every role I've occupied as an adult. Through this experience, I learned the power of mentoring, which has given me a great passion for engaging the younger generation of citizens. Exchanging ideas and points of view with a group of millennial entrepreneurs, artists, and business owners on a regular basis keeps me energized about the future, and it inspires me to continue to work toward fulfilling our country's vast potential. For my younger friends, I provide a sounding board and am able to share some of my own lessons learned through my time in business as well as in the public sector. At the end of the day, it's simply a win/win situation.

A recent study showed that 79 percent of millennials believe "mentorship programs are crucial to their career success."[1] When you consider that by the year 2025, 75 percent of the workforce will be millennials, this is a statistic we should all keep in mind as we seek to grow our businesses as well as our communities. Fostering new leadership through the mentoring process isn't just some warm, fuzzy idea; it's a key principle in ensuring that our workplaces and the places we call home are able to recruit and retain the lifeblood of the best and brightest young minds.

## Millennials: Natural-Born Changemakers

Over the past several years I've developed great friendships and working relationships with many young leaders throughout our

---

1    Missy Chicre, "How Millennials Can Benefit from Mentoring," Menttium, accessed February 21, 2019, https://www.menttium.com/ millennials-can-benefit-mentoring/.

community. They're entrepreneurs, CEOs of successful technology start-ups, restaurant owners, vice presidents of successful companies, and elected officials who share in common the fact that they're all under the age of forty.

My radio show was born out of a gig sitting in as guest host on another show, where I featured leaders who are dynamic, forward thinking, and passionately engaged in simply making the world a better place. Two of the team members I had helping me on the show, Virginia Claussen, who worked with my consulting firm, and Bethany Davis, who co-hosted our Midweek Music Mashup featuring live local music, are millennials themselves and contributed to us breaking through to the younger generation of Augustans. In getting to know this generation, I've come to admire their "we first" style of leadership, where they don't view their own individual successes as a competition to outdo each other, but rather see them as a collective victory which they can all be proud of. A refreshing mind-set to say the least when I've witnessed firsthand how a "me-first" style of leadership can stifle progress in organizations and cities alike.

In developing these strong ties to millennials, I've concluded that these folks are natural-born Changemakers. First off, they are motivated and creative problem-solvers, who would rather act than form a committee to address any issue they encounter. Simply put, they are doers and not talkers, and

In developing these strong ties to millennials, I've concluded that these folks are natural-born Changemakers.

having served as mayor for nine years, I can speak from experience in saying that I certainly would have liked to have worked with more people who were willing to roll up their sleeves and get things done as opposed to forming another study committee.

Another quality that millennials and Changemakers share is that this generation of leaders has developed a much more global mind-set as opposed to the provincial mind-set held by some in leadership positions who came before them. Remember, this is a generation where social networking has long been a part of their daily lives, which has resulted in them seeing themselves as being part of a much larger online community while exposing them to different cultures and different ways of thinking throughout their formative years.

Finally, they're team players, who don't seem to let their egos get in the way of accomplishing their collective goals. As I mentioned earlier, their "we-first" mentality has certainly helped lead them to great successes early in life, as they've always helped to lift each other to greater heights. Having witnessed politics firsthand for many years, I can attest to the fact that municipal governments everywhere could use more team players at the elected level focused on serving the greater good of their cities as a whole as opposed to focusing on simply serving their own particular districts or constituencies.

Millennials are extremely bright, they're extremely active, and they have a strong social conscience. As compared to my generation, Generation X, with all its stereotypical angst and anxiety, they're also a whole lot more optimistic and enthusiastic about the future than past generations and that enthusiasm is contagious.

With all this in mind and with the amazing, constantly developing skill sets this generation brings to the table, I believe its undoubtedly time that organizations at all levels give them a stronger voice in the decision-making process. However, if we as leaders are going to do this, it can't be to placate or pacify this generation as we tell them we value their input but to wait patiently at the children's table until it's their turn to lead.

Each generation is unique and becomes romanticized to some degree or another over time. However, I truly believe that, in a world full of unique challenges growing exponentially at an ever-increasing pace, the millennial generation has the talent and ability to meet these challenges head on. I also believe they will do this faster if the generations that came before them, mine included, realize this massive potential and go ahead and give them that seat at the grown-up's table.

> I truly believe that, in a world full of unique challenges growing exponentially at an ever-increasing pace, the millennial generation has the talent and ability to meet these challenges head on.

I encourage you to take a look at the seven attributes of Changemakers again, with the millennial generation in mind: Creativity, Courage, Connecting, Listening, Transparency, Composure, and Character. All these things are hallmarks of what we consider millennials.

They listen. They care. And they have empathy, a critical skill in raising your emotional intelligence (EI).

## The Art of EI

So, what is EI? For those unfamiliar with the concept, it's "the capability of individuals to recognize their own emotions and those of others, discern between different feelings and label them appropriately, use emotional information to guide thinking and behavior, and manage and/or adjust emotions to adapt to environments or achieve one's goal(s). Studies have shown that people with high EI have greater mental health, job performance, and leadership skills."[2]

It's about understanding our own thoughts and feelings and realizing the affect our behaviors have on others. It's about having empathy for others, which can only come from listening. More and more businesses are actually adopting best-practice models for raising the EI of their employees, especially the leaders of the organization, with tremendous results.

## So how do you raise your EI? Learn to listen without prejudice.

So how do you raise your EI? Learn to listen without prejudice.

We've all been in the situation where we can't wait to jump into a conversation to interject our own perspective based on our *perceived* notion that what's just come out of someone's mouth is flat-out wrong.

Even if we can wait our turn to speak, our hearts begin to beat a bit faster, our mind races with potential responses to the offending party, and when we finally do respond we introduce our personal biases into the mix based on our own life experiences. Nine times out of ten, this leads to an argument, whether the topic is sports, politics, music, business, or someone's own particular fashion sense. I've watched it happen, I've been a part of it … and admit it, so have you.

As I told my friend Chris, the good Lord gave us two eyes, two ears, and one mouth, which says to me that we should probably consider spending two thirds of our time watching and listening and a third of it talking. Easier said than done, particularly when we have something we *really, really* want to say.

---

2    "Emotional Intelligence," Wikipedia, accessed February 21, 2019, https://en.wikipedia.org/wiki/Emotional_intelligence.

Listening without prejudice and learning to hold our tongue can be done … and here's how:

## 1. Use the Thirty-Second Rule

In the heat of the moment, it's so easy to let our tongues slip and say something we might regret later. Rather than releasing your tongue in anger or in haste when someone says something you feel isn't correct, take a deep breath and count to thirty. Remember it takes much more strength to hold your tongue in patience than to release it in anger. And the results of learning to do this effectively help to keep you cool under pressure whatever the situation may be.

## 2. Consider the other person's point of view

We've all been socialized in different ways which lead us to have unique perspectives on life, which isn't a bad thing. Just because someone has a different point of view from your own doesn't make them bad or wrong. It just makes them different. You may not agree with some peoples' points of view, but just taking a moment to consider them may give you a different perspective on why they feel the way they do.

## 3. Consider what you would say if there were children in the room

During my nine years as a public servant, I always reminded my colleagues that children might be watching our actions during any given meeting. Keeping that thought at the forefront of my mind oftentimes stopped me from saying things I would probably have liked to but that were ultimately better left unsaid. Even though we're not all in the public eye in our business or personal relationships, this is still a good rule of thumb to use to avoid saying something to another person that you definitely wouldn't say in front of a child.

## 4. Imagine your conversation is being recorded

In today's world where privacy is becoming a thing of the past, it's not a real stretch to think that anything you say may end up being recorded. When you're tempted to let loose and say something you probably shouldn't, take a moment to think about your words being recorded and put online where they could be played for a worldwide audience on a continual loop. Thinking about things that way usually helps to keep your ears open and your mouth closed.

## 5. Remember what your mother always told you: be polite!

In a world that seems to get less and less civil every day, there's simply something refreshing about a polite listener who takes the time to hear what others have to say. This is definitely a character trait that can be developed over time and something that contributes immeasurably to good communication skills. Plus, being a polite listener would make your mother proud, so why not do it, right?

Becoming a good, open-minded listener is undoubtedly not rocket science. But it does take time, effort, and self-discipline. However, to be able to really listen to others without interjecting your own preconceived notions into the conversation is one of the most important aspects of becoming a truly great communicator ... and a Changemaker.

**Becoming a good, open-minded listener is undoubtedly not rocket science. But it does take time, effort, and self-discipline.**

## TWO CENTS FOR CHANGE

Let's face it, we live in a world full of noise where the volume seems to be increasing by the minute. And truly listening through all the distractions presented to us on a daily basis is no easy task. However, being a good listener is undoubtedly a fundamental key to becoming a changemaker.

1. Can you remember the last meeting you participated in where you listened much more than you talked? I used the listening lesson my father taught me while running our local commission meetings as expeditiously as possible. My job, as a I saw it, was to continue to keep the meetings moving and interjecting my own voice into the conversation only when necessary.

2. When was the last time, in a personal or professional setting, where you immediately regretted what you said verbally or electronically? I made the point in an earlier chapter that the art of communication seems to be becoming a dying art, and our lightning-fast forms of communication, although great in some respects, aren't helping the problem. Whether it's releasing your tongue in anger or frustration or hitting the send button with the same mind-set, always remember that once your words are conveyed, the damage control is usually way more painful than not letting them go in the first place.

3. Have you ever misread a situation due to your unwillingness to listen? I've often seen this happen when someone is interrupted prior to being given a chance to get their point across. I've found it's easy to misread situations and hard to come up with solutions if you don't have all the information in front of you before making a decision. It

may take a little longer to hear someone out, but taking that extra little bit of time usually gives you a much better read on situations. As my wife taught me when we were first married, I was more focused on trying to fix problems than I was on just listening to her.

4.  When was the last time you had a conversation with someone and an hour later you could barely remember what you had talked about? We live in a fast world where we're constantly bombarded with information, and it can often be a little hard to keep up. One thing I've found to be helpful is to try not to multi-task when I'm having a conversation. As tied as we may be to our cell phones and other devices, they can definitely be a distraction from the listening process.

5.  When was the last time you thanked someone for telling you what you wanted to hear and not what you needed to hear? While I was running the Augusta Economic Development Authority on an interim basis, several board members encouraged me to apply for the position of president of the organization. I use my friend and former executive assistant, Karyn, as a sounding board, so I ran the idea by her. She shared with me her opinion that I had been tied down in office for nine years and filling that role on a full-time basis would effectively create the same situation. At first, I was a little offended and my ego was a bit bruised. But her input made me also realize that, despite my experience with economic development, I was not a highly trained professional that the organization needed at a critical juncture. After thinking it through and discussing it with Malisa, I realized she was right and thanked her for telling me what I needed to hear as opposed to what I wanted to hear.

chapter seven

# Transparency: Be Vulnerable

*Opening yourself up to the world around you means knowingly exposing yourself to life's great challenges. But it's the only way to connect with and lead others in a profound and lasting manner.*

**—DEKE COPENHAVER**

It was March 16, 2010. I had been in a meeting, and when I came out of my office, Karyn told me that TMZ Sports had just called looking for me. My first question to her was, "Does TMZ even cover sports?" The reality of the situation was that Tiger Woods had recently announced that the first tournament he would be playing in, following his personal scandal in 2009, was the Masters. Several years earlier, I had met Tiger under a very interesting set of circumstances. I had just dropped my father-in-law off at the clubhouse at the Augusta National before parking in a designated parking zone. While heading to the tournament, I'd seen Tiger and noticed he had no entourage around him. So, I asked a security guard if it would be alright if I stopped by to welcome Tiger to Augusta. The guard let me through, and I went on to greet him and wish him the best in that year's Masters. Later, I passed by that same security guard who told me: "He got the biggest kick out of that. You just made Tiger Woods smile, my friend!" I remember thinking at that moment how strange and amazing my life was. Somehow, I'd made one of the greatest golfers of all time smile. Just surreal.

Having had that moment with Tiger, I was somewhat taken aback by the current set of circumstances. But at the same time, I saw an opportunity. I shared with Karyn that we would use this newfound attention to give a well-rounded perspective of the city we love. We have always been blessed to be the only permanent home of a major golf tournament, but there's so much more to our community. And we decided to showcase it in the national and international media sensation that surrounded Tiger's announcement. We determined immediately that if at all possible, we would do all interviews from our city center.

Interestingly, most of the reporters remarked that they had no idea we had such a charming downtown—including those from just two hours away in Atlanta. The world pictured Augusta as an eighteen-hole golf course that we're undoubtedly blessed to be home to, but we wanted to show them more and to use an international media opportunity to highlight that our community had much more to offer than just golf. During the tournament, my week culminated with a live interview with Bloomberg News to share the great strides we had made in our local economy in the midst of the Great Recession. Ultimately, we were able to leverage a great opportunity by simply being open to the possibilities presented to us in a unique moment in history. And in retrospect, having had my life intersect for a brief moment with Tiger's has given me an even greater appreciation for the way he has fought with and overcome adversity in his own life.

> Changemakers *need* to realize and be open and vulnerable to the opportunities around them.

Changemakers *need* to realize and be open and vulnerable to the opportunities around them. They have to be on the ground, in the trenches, whether it's at a major golf tournament or in the major events of life.

## Empty the Ivory Tower

If you're trying to effect change, there's no sequestering yourself from the people you're trying to serve. You can't live in an ivory tower. The fact is, if you're not present, you're perceived as hollow.

I've discussed my distaste for painting people with a broad brush. Well, that phenomenon works both ways. I remember once when I visited one of our inner-city schools. Invariably, kids will ask the most interesting questions. One young man raised his hand. "Do you have a limo?" I laughed and said, "No, I don't have a limo. The president of the United States needs a limo for security reasons, but I don't need a limo. I drive myself just like everybody else. And I don't have any bodyguards either." He couldn't believe it. "What?!

You don't have a limo?" I shook my head. "No, I just don't roll like that." He seemed to think about my answer for a moment. Then he asked, "Why not? Don't you want a limo?"

I couldn't help but think how unfortunate it was that a young man had that perception of politicians, of leaders. That they are elitists, sitting in their ivory towers and riding around in limousines, above everyone else. That's just not a good impression for the next generation to have of leadership. True leaders need to have a presence in order to effect change. There is no way to change things if you are out of touch with the conditions people live in.

## Changing Perception

I didn't conceive the general idea of what the average man on the street perceives a politician to be. When I first ran for office, I realized not everybody in the city knew me. As a matter of fact, I was pretty much an unknown. But I couldn't understand why there were people who had never even met me who hated me. I came to realize that it was the negative perception of politics and politicians in general. And even though I didn't perceive myself as a typical politician, to many of the constituents I served, there were preconceived notions about what a politician was.

> Even though I didn't perceive myself as a typical politician, to many of the constituents I served, there were preconceived notions about what a politician was.

When I took office, the approval rating for our commission was 22 percent. I've always focused on team building, and you have to be open to build a team. Team building takes building trust in your team and admitting you don't have all the answers, even if you're leading the team. You have to share your vulnerability.

In my first year in office, I decided early on to take the commission to a retreat, based on the suggestions of commissioners who'd been there before me and shared that there had not been a retreat in years. Due to listening to people who had much more experience than me, basically we started team-building right then and there. It wasn't my idea, but it was a good idea, and I give credit to the commissioners for a suggestion that paid dividends, in spite of the fact we may have had a difference of opinions on a number of issues. As we entered the retreat, I shared the approval rating of the commission during my campaign. "The approval rating of this body is 22 percent, and I'm now part of this body. I don't know about you guys, but if I'm on a team, I want to be on a winning team." I actually had a commissioner who happened to be a coach say that 22 percent was better than the approval rating for Congress. I said, "How you can be satisfied with a 22 percent approval rating? I'm sorry if you feel that way, but I'm not."

Seeking to build on the team-building effort of the retreat, we arranged a bus tour to visit every single commission district, so that commissioners from certain districts who had probably never been in other districts were able to actually see the conditions that people lived in. They could share the strengths and weaknesses and the issues, and ultimately it built a stronger connection within the body. It gave everybody a real-world idea of the issues that their colleagues in any single district were facing. In all honesty, I simply used the model of Leadership Georgia, where a group of leaders from all over Georgia spend a year traveling around the state learning the challenges and successes in our individual communities.

Legendary Charleston, South Carolina mayor, Joe Riley, a friend and mentor and a Changemaker if ever there was one, once made a remark during a speech which resonates with me to this very day. He pointed out that all too often elected officials in local governments get bogged down in petty arguments where in six months no one will remember what the argument was about. He then went on to say that if elected officials will focus on building things together, this is what will stand the test of time. I'm proud to say that working with my elected colleagues together we were able to build a new convention center, a new judicial center, a new library, and a new law-enforcement center during our season as public servants. It was truly a team effort, and I believe it all started with our team-building efforts in my first year in office.

Over time, having had nine years in office to really get to know people and to spend time with them throughout the community, I believe I changed the perception of politicians in our community. By the end of my term, there were people who initially didn't know me and didn't trust me, but by being open and being present with the people I served, and with a lot of relationship building, I was able to turn around that negative connotation of what a politician was.

## Strength in Vulnerability

Having grown up in the South, raised by parents who grew up in small towns in Virginia, I have a deep understanding of the idea of keeping a stiff upper lip and soldiering on in the face of adversity while not "airing your dirty laundry." I respect that idea, but I also see that it can be a faulty mind-set to adhere to. Although I was once a shy kid from Canada, my roots run deep in a culture that I value for its strength, resiliency, and gentility. However, I also understand it's a culture that's not at all without its inherent issues, same as with any other culture. In our culture, as within many others worldwide, vulnerability is often seen as weakness, while openly and honestly discussing issues we're facing as individuals, businesses, families, and communities seems to never be an easy conversation to have. While dealing with Kellie's illness in my twenties, I had experienced firsthand the toll that keeping a stiff upper lip and not reaching out to loved ones during the difficult times in life can have on you.

The truth is we all have issues and insecurities we deal with on a daily basis, which ultimately makes us all vulnerable and, as much as we don't like to admit it at times, human. But something we can all learn is that our common vulnerability can be used as a strength, because admitting you have it binds us together in that it begins to build trust with each other. Changemakers have to be willing to let their guard down as opposed to putting up walls in their efforts to create lasting positive change. But a word to the wise: opening up and letting your guard down in your changemaking efforts often brings you face to face with one of the essential human conditions no one can ever avoid—hurt.

> Changemakers have to be willing to let their guard down as opposed to putting up walls in their efforts to create lasting positive change.

I've often said that artists and musicians are natural-born Changemakers because of their inherent need to share themselves and be vulnerable. They are some of the most beautiful souls, and oftentimes they're the most broken souls because of the world of raw emotion in which they live. The courage it takes for artists to perform, to open themselves up to critics and cynics, to put their art out there for the world to see and judge is what a Changemaker is all about, whether it's a musician or a visual artist or a sculptor or a writer.

Phillip Lee, a great friend of mine whom I was mentoring, took his life at twenty-nine years old in August of 2018. He was a very talented musician, a tremendous athlete, and just an amazing human being. We had actually made a deal during a round of golf earlier that year: if he'd help me improve my golf game, I'd train him to be Augusta's first rock star mayor. His charismatic personality drew people to him like moths to a flame, and his big heart, love for people, and his willingness to give of himself to those he loved was an amazing thing to behold. In high school, he was the star quarterback on the football team and star pitcher on the baseball team whom all the girls loved. However, after college he chose a different path and decided to pursue a career as a professional musician with a great deal of success along the way. But unfortunately, as with many creatively gifted individuals, he dealt with mental health issues which led to him self-medicating. His mental and emotional decline had come on swiftly, but after having lunch together two weeks before it happened, I was still very hopeful he was making progress in dealing with his issues through his faith and through his strong support system led by his loving family. I told Malisa shortly after hearing the news of his passing: "You know, it hurts like hell to lose somebody so close to you. It's just plain painful. But I wouldn't trade the pleasure of getting to know him for never having known him at all. I'm blessed to call him *friend.*"

Phillip helped me with my strong connection to our local music community. And that connection helped me comfort them, along with Phillip's family, during what was a very personal loss for all involved. Having dealt with the pain of my wife and many friends taking their own lives provided a connection to those grieving his passing, of which I was one. Growing up with a true appreciation for the way arts and music bring people together connected me to our local arts community. That's what connected me to Phillip—a shared love of music, family, friends, and our community.

We have to open ourselves up to other people as Changemakers, but we are going to find some hurt there, too. That's okay. You have to have the courage to understand that it's almost a ministry to be a Changemaker. You have to console people and encourage them, and although it can, at times, be emotionally draining, it's also rewarding. When you are willing to let your guard down, you're dropping your defenses and you're asking someone else to drop their defenses as well. You're going to expose scars and you're going to see scars. You're going to see wounds that may still need to heal. But for others to open themselves to you, you need to make them feel protected and secure in doing so.

Changemakers must open up their hearts and their spirits and their lives to people from many walks of life to make that kind of connection. However, having a willingness to not keep their guard up means it's inevitable that Changemakers are going to get hurt. The more people you open up yourself to, the more likely you are to lose somebody. At the same time, you have to have the courage to understand that going in. If you want to truly effect change in your organization or in your community, you

> If you want to truly effect change in your organization or in your community, you can't do it unless you're intersecting with many different lives ... and that can only be done if you're willing to be unguarded and open.

can't do it unless you're intersecting with many different lives … and that can only be done if you're willing to be unguarded and open.

## Authenticity Speaks Volumes

Being a Changemaker is certainly not easy. Being asked to speak at the funerals of your friends and loved ones is not easy, because you're emotionally raw as well. Not that you ever welcome the opportunity, but sometimes to be a leader, a Changemaker, you have to be the one willing to set the tone in any given situation. You have to have an authentic connection with people to be able to impact change.

Freddie, the husband of Carolyn Smith, a dear friend who has worked with us for years and who we consider a part of our family, passed away in September of 2017. To join in honoring his passing, Malisa and I attended the service at Newhope Missionary Baptist Church, a large African-American church here in Augusta. When we got there, they made the announcement of the speakers. Although I wasn't listed on the program and had not been informed, they announced that the former mayor, that being me, was going to be a speaker.

Fortunately, they put me last, so I had a few minutes to think. Malisa leaned over to me and said, "Did you know that you're speaking?" I let her know that I had no clue, but I was able to get up and speak about Freddie, and afterwards the crowd overwhelmingly said how much they appreciated my words about their family member and friend.

A Changemaker doesn't need to always be polished and prepared, just authentic.

> A Changemaker doesn't need to always be polished and prepared, just authentic.

I can't imagine anyone who *wants* to be known as a funeral speaker, but to have people who you know, or sometimes people you don't know for that matter, hoping for you to say a few words on behalf of their loved one is a very powerful thing. I've actually become the go-to writer for obituaries in our family. Being able to capture the memory of those individuals, whether it's in spoken word or written word, is a privilege and an honor.

If you have a chance to speak to a graduating class of kindergarteners or the honor to be asked to speak at someone's funeral, you've earned the authenticity of a Changemaker.

## The Taste of Humble Pie

But one word of caution: Changemakers aren't perfect. There was a situation where we were trying to hire a new administrator in 2014. The process was that the city advertised the position, then the mayor culled through the applications and presented the three top candidates to the commission to be interviewed. The mayor made a recommendation regarding who to hire, but the commission could still hire whichever candidate they wanted. The most qualified candidate in my opinion was a gentleman by the name of Oscar Rodriguez. After the interview process, I met with the commissioners and had assurances that they were ready to approve Mr. Rodriguez. But when we came down to voting on it, they weren't willing to vote on my recommended candidate and voted to simply scrap the process. It was very frustrating to me, because it had been a lengthy process, and I'd taken the time to meet with individuals and shore up the votes to get approval for the man I truly believed was the most qualified candidate—meaning no offense to any of the other candidates.

That week, we were having the premiere for the James Brown biopic *Get on Up* in Augusta, and I had offered two tickets to a commissioner who ended up not voting for my candidate. I told him, "You're not getting the tickets now." I immediately knew I'd done the wrong thing, so I left the tickets in will-call for him, but he didn't use them. Naturally, this hit the press and became a public issue. Ironically, the most feedback I got was that I should have lost my cool with him years before—and people were applauding me for what I knew had been the wrong decision. Once again, no one is perfect, but I felt like I needed to make a bad decision right. In a subsequent commission meeting, I publicly apologized to him. That was a humbling feeling, but I realized I'd done the wrong thing. I let my anger get the best of me, and I owed him an apology, so I did it publicly. And rest assured that was not the only time I had to publicly swallow my pride.

> Humility is strength and is a key trait of a true leader. If you really want to be a Changemaker and master the art of leadership, it takes a humbleness of spirit.

We still have a good relationship, even several years out of office. But I had to humble myself to do that. Sometimes people perceive humility to be a weakness. Not so. Humility is strength and is a key trait of a true leader. If you really want to be a Changemaker and master the art of leadership, it takes a humbleness of spirit.

Believe it or not, no one's ever choked to death on swallowing pride.

# Humor Me

A number of years ago, while I was still in office, I was scheduled to attend our annual United Way luncheon. On my way out of the office as I headed to the event, I asked Karyn Nixon, my executive assistant at the time, "So what am I doing at the luncheon?" She told me that it was no big deal, and that I was just bringing greetings. When I got to the luncheon, I was seated on the dais. Prior to the luncheon beginning, all the guests seated on the dais were introduced to the crowd with a live shot of them flashed up on the big screen. Shortly thereafter, I was introduced as the keynote speaker for the event. To open my remarks, I shared with the audience that the terrified look on my face they'd seen during my introduction came because I had only just realized that I was the keynote speaker. After letting them in on the joke, I told them, "And hopefully I won't suck, but here goes!" The crowd erupted in laughter, I was set at ease, and the speech went on to be a great success. When using humor, honesty is always the best policy!

**When using humor, honesty is always the best policy!**

# Going Off Script

When I met with the ForbesBooks team in Charleston, South Carolina, I shared with them that I always speak extemporaneously. Their eyes said it all. "Even for your TEDx talk?" I replied, "Yes, even for my TEDx talk." Needless to say, they seemed a bit shocked.

You see, before you get through a TEDx, they want to know exactly what you're going to say and ask you to submit it in writing. "I don't know exactly what I'm going to say," I told my assigned coach, who was completely freaking out. But ultimately he had to trust me. Fortunately, it worked out and I didn't fall off the front of the stage. In fact, it had the desired impact, as the words I spoke about cities being places where all things connect resonated with the audience and were very well received. And to be perfectly honest, I think if I had to actually write and rehearse a speech I'd probably trip over my words and fall flat on my face in the process.

To be a Changemaker inherently means to do things differently. If you do things differently, you're going to be shunned by some and not understood by others. Yet to be able to open up and speak extemporaneously allows you to connect with your audience in a way that you can never connect through a scripted speech.

The bottom line: being a Changemaker means going off script.

## The Art of Being Transparent

In a world where trust of those in leadership positions is at an absolute premium, being transparent is one of the most fundamental tools for building this trust and maximizing your impact as a decision-maker.

> Being transparent is one of the most fundamental tools for building this trust and maximizing your impact as a decision-maker.

Whether you're building a business, embarking on a foray into public service, or crusading for a cause you're passionate about, trust in your leadership and your brand matters and once its undermined, its next to impossible to re-establish.

During my time as a public servant, I realized early on the importance of information flow and the key role living a life online and in the public eye played in getting a message across to the people

I served. I also realized that having a major online presence and the media spotlight afforded me the opportunity to be as transparent as possible while building a strong level of public trust which contributed greatly to our citizenry re-electing me every time I ran.

A daily focus on being as transparent as possible in a leadership position is not an easy thing to achieve, as it creates a level of perceived accessibility which simply didn't exist in previous generations and can at times be hard to maintain. However, if handled correctly, being a transparent and accessible leader in any position you may hold will ultimately pay extraordinary dividends.

With this in mind, here are five ways which should help you become more transparent in your leadership position while building bonds of trust with the people you serve.

## 1. Be authentic

In focusing on being transparent in leadership positions, always remember to be authentic. Whether it be online, on TV, on the radio, or in person, it's important that the voice the people you serve or work with hear is yours and isn't coming from a script or someone responding for you.

## 2. Be proactive

A large part of being transparent in leadership positions is to be proactive in getting information out there. In a world where most of us have become our own news sources, leaders of any organization have the opportunity to provide good information and accurate content to the people they serve daily. Keeping those you serve or work with in the loop on a regular basis helps create a sense of openness while fostering a greater sense of trust in your leadership.

## 3. Be accurate

In a world where leaders are forced to fight a constant battle with misinformation, making absolutely certain that any information you share with those you serve is accurate is an absolute must. Even if the information you're sharing is not good news, its vitally important that those in leadership positions paint a clear picture of any situation that may have an impact on their team or organization.

## 4. Be prepared

Focusing on being a transparent leader means being prepared to handle the tough questions, as they're always going to come if you maintain your openness and accessibility. Whether it be in front of your employees, your citizens, or the media, it's never a good thing for people in leadership positions to get caught like a deer in head-lights. Anticipating the tough questions ahead of time goes a long way toward helping you to answer them as opposed to dodging them and undermining trust in your leadership.

## 5. Be honest

As simple as this may sound, it is absolutely the most essential part of being a transparent leader and building trust in those you serve in whatever capacity that may be. Being honest and sharing information with your team, your organization, or your citizens that they need to hear as opposed to telling them what you think they want to hear can be difficult at times. However, it's simply the right thing to do and is the best way to build trust in your leadership.

When our society is now at a point where people are hungrier than they've ever been for accurate information and strong leadership, being an accessible, open, and transparent leader is more important than ever in fostering a sense of trust in your leadership.

Ultimately, a commitment to be a Changemaker means having to work a little harder and to go the extra mile when it comes to being open and building trust. However, it's always been my experience that if people trust you, they'll work with you, and in the end the success in whatever leadership position you may occupy is never achieved by any one given individual, but rather is the result of a true team effort.

# For Phillip

*We found ourselves in a time and place,*
*Where together we could share.*
*To you I was a mentor,*
*To me you were fresh air.*
*In the times we spent together,*
*I came to know your heart.*
*Spaceless, timeless, loving care,*
*Your life a work of art.*
*You touched the soul of a city,*
*A place your heart called home.*
*You inspired countless masses,*
*While your spirit called you to roam.*
*Through music we connected,*
*Sharing a bond so real and true.*
*And God gave us an angel,*
*When he blessed our lives through you.*
*Love, Deke*
*September 10, 2018*

**TWO CENTS FOR CHANGE**

Being open and transparent can be one of the greatest challenges we can face in leadership positions, in both our personal and professional lives. The natural impulse toward self-preservation and often not wanting to own the most difficult situations facing our families, our businesses, and our communities can become stifling to our personal and professional growth. Becoming a Changemaker and a better leader always has an element of facing our own fears head on.

1. Have you ever had to open up and face one of your greatest fears head on? Several years ago, I was invited to participate in the Ronald MacDonald House "Over the Edge" fundraiser, where local leaders were asked to rappel down the side of a ten story building. I'm definitely not a fan of heights, but wearing the Spiderman costume Malisa had insisted I wear because it was Halloween, I made it down. I also drenched the costume in sweat during my descent.

2. In a leadership position, have you ever admitted publicly or to your team that you made the wrong decision? Unfortunately, we all make bad decisions—in life and in leadership—and that's okay, as long as we're willing to own up to them. Pride can be a major issue to deal with for a lot of us, and the faster we learn to swallow it, the better off we are.

3. As a leader, have you ever delegated your messaging to someone else? I know that we live in an extremely busy world where social networking in particular can be extremely time consuming. However, in order to be authentic, always

remember that in order to have a maximum impact, your words have to be your own.

4.  In your role as a leader, do you make transparency a priority? While in office, I had an open-door policy for the public, the press, and my elected colleagues. I didn't have anyone screening who came to see me, and my door was literally always open unless I was in a meeting. Remember, open doors build trust while closed doors build suspicion. And being approachable is a critical attribute of transparency and becoming a better leader.

5.  In your leadership position, have you surrounded yourself with a team you can trust? Changemaking leadership is hard, and maintaining a calm exterior when you're dealing your own doubts or fears in the midst of life's storms is never easy. Surrounding yourself with people you can trust, whom you can open up to, and who appreciate your own vulnerabilities, is an absolute key to creating lasting change.

chapter eight

# Composure:
# Keep Calm and Lead On

*The role of a good leader in crisis is to set the tone for others
to follow and to become the calm at the center of the storm.*

**—DEKE COPENHAVER**

I love the following picture of French General Charles de Gaulle. My
mom actually had a huge crush on him from watching film footage
of how cool he remained under pressure. That's the hallmark of a
Changemaker, and of what people look for in a leader. It's easy to lead
when things are quiet and stable. But it's another thing altogether

to lead when things aren't going well, when tragedy strikes, when adversity hits, when there's great loss, when there's poverty, when there's war.

Being the leader of any organization or community puts you in a position where controversy is a place you live; when it arises, you're always in the middle of it. Adversity had started for me on day one in office, and it never let up over nine years.

Several months after our nation's economic meltdown hit with the Great Recession of fall, 2008, the Obama administration passed the largest spending package in our nation's history: the American Recovery and Reinvestment Act, also known as the Stimulus Package, in order to stimulate the American economy. Cities were eligible to receive funding for a multitude of different projects, which to sum up here would make my head spin. Suffice it to say that Augusta was eligible for, and applied for, millions of dollars in federal grant funding. Unfortunately, federal legislation on such a massive, wide-reaching scale led to a constantly moving target of rules and everchanging

> Being the leader of any organization or community puts you in a position where controversy is a place you live; when it arises, you're always in the middle of it.

deadlines just to apply for the funding. In trying to hit one of those moving targets based upon a request from our Housing and Neighborhood Development director—a man I had worked with for years and trusted—I signed off on a grant application. In an effort to not put the funding opportunity in jeopardy, I did this *without* receiving the approval of the commission. Had we gone through our regular process to approve grant applications, we would have simply missed the deadline. Needless to say, my colleagues on the commission weren't happy with me.

Ultimately, $30 million of the funding had been set aside to help redevelop a large tract of land adjacent to Goshen Country Club, a golf-course community, into a mixed-use development, much like the Eastlake neighborhood housing the Drew Charter School in Atlanta, which I highlighted in an earlier chapter. Basically, as I saw it, my belief in the mixed-use model had led me to try to make something good happen in the midst of a financial catastrophe for our nation. However, not everyone shared my point of view.

The backlash was immediate, as local elected officials fanned the flames of the neighborhood association for not being informed ahead of time, even though, based on the rules we were given by the federal government, this was literally impossible. A neighborhood association meeting was held to address the issue, which to describe as heated would be an understatement. I was given an opportunity to address the crowd, to try to explain to them the circumstances that put us in the situation in the first place. It was raucous out of the gates. I stopped for a minute and said, "I feel like I'm at a health care reform town hall meeting." The crowd erupted with shouts and applause. I then said, "Or on the Jerry Springer Show." In retrospect, I probably should have held my tongue on that last one. As you can imagine, the reception was not a good one. And having that be the headline on the eleven o'clock news wasn't what I was had hoped for. But the important takeaway is that I had remained calm and stood my ground in front of an angry crowd, and in the midst of controversy.

In the end, the fears and concerns of the people living in Goshen were completely understandable given the heightened sense of anxiety facing our entire nation at the point in time. I respected them for the stand they took in spite of my own opinion to support such a unique redevelopment opportunity for their neighborhood, one that likely wouldn't come along again in the foreseeable future.

Ultimately, the neighborhood association and the elected officials who saw an opportunity to curry favor with voters got their victory with the grant application being pulled. Although I could have jumped on the political bandwagon and scored political points in the process, I still believe that remaining calm and not fanning the flames is always the best course of action when your focus is on changemaking leadership. In the end, you may lose some battles along the way by calmly staying the course, but remaining consistent tends to win the wars we face both in life and in leadership.

You may lose some battles along the way by calmly staying the course, but remaining consistent tends to win the wars we face both in life and in leadership.

Being a better leader simply calls for maintaining your composure in whatever challenging situation you may face. And exposing yourself to trials by fire is a good thing. I always viewed every situation dealing with controversies as an exercise in my ability to maintain my composure and maintain a cool, calm, and steady approach to leading our city during that season of my life.

I didn't grow up wanting to be mayor. And I sure didn't think I was going to be mayor of Augusta during the passing of James Brown, or during the worst recession in my lifetime, or during the most devastating storm that our community had ever seen. But it's that kind of trial by fire—and learning how to keep your composure in the midst of the storm—that makes a leader effective and impactful. As the point of the spear, whether you're a CEO or a mayor, people are looking to you, judging your reaction. Think about the three-year-old who runs down the sidewalk and suddenly trips and skins his knee. What's the first thing he does? He looks right at the parents for their reaction. If the parent shows panic and concern, the child will likely cry. If the parent is calm and soothing, the child is apt to get back up and start running again without missing a beat.

So, during the recession and the storm of the century and some of the contentious political battles I've faced, I always maintained a level of calm, and it gave strength to the people around me. As a Changemaker, if you do not maintain your composure, you're not going to effect the change you're trying to implement.

> As a Changemaker, if you do not maintain your composure, you're not going to effect the change you're trying to implement.

## Getting in Your Head

In any sporting event, things can happen, and people get heated. Maybe there is trash talk, or maybe a fight breaks out. If you notice, though, most professional athletes somehow find a calmness within, a peace, a center to be able to get back in the game and focus on getting the job done. In the world of sports, it's simply referred to as "getting in the zone." The fact is, you can't sustain playing angry. You're not going to continue to make baskets or hit homeruns if you continually lose your head. But that's the point. There are people out there who want to get into your head, who want you to lose your cool, especially when you're in a leadership position.

If people can get in your head or under your skin, then *they* are suddenly controlling the situation. They're manipulating you. I'm an extremely competitive person, and I don't like to be manipulated. I've found you actually get more done by ignoring the temptation to lose your cool and instead just maintain your composure. It establishes a boundary and gives the people around you a message that the space inside your head is not for rent.

## The Sport of Mudslinging

Political campaigns nowadays come with the negative ads, the mudslinging against one candidate or the other. Most passive viewers take those ads as a tactic in trying to frame a certain picture of the candidate in a negative light, so that voters take that impression of the candidate to the polls. But the fact is, those ads are also trying to get a reaction, a negative reaction, out of the respective opponent. Maybe that opponent loses his or her cool and spouts off and says something controversial in an interview or on Twitter.

> Real leadership, the kind it takes to be a Changemaker, requires you to set the tone and remain calm, even in political campaigns.

Real leadership, the kind it takes to be a Changemaker, requires you to set the tone and remain calm, even in political campaigns. I'm proud to say that, generally, the campaigns I ran in didn't become mudslinging affairs. How was that possible? Because I made sure not only as a candidate, but as a city mayor, to set the tone.

Earlier in the book, I mentioned the church leadership retreat that I went on the year I first ran for office. Well, the moderator there also made it a point to set the tone for the retreat. He told a story about when he was young and had gotten into a fight at school. Apparently, he went home and said to his mother, "It wasn't my fault. There wouldn't have been a fight at all if he hadn't hit me." To which his mother replied, "No, there wouldn't have been a fight if you hadn't hit him *back*."

I had another great friend who was a minister, and once in a sermon he said "So if you're driving your car and a dog starts to chase you, what do you do? You just keep driving. So, in life, if your hands are clean and your heart is pure, let people say what they want and keep driving."

People may have said things about me, but I never reacted to them; I just didn't take the bait. To be a Changemaker, you have to be able to keep your cool and can't take their bait. And believe me, people will want to get you off your game, but if your hands are clean and your heart is pure, just keep on driving.

> So, in life, if your hands are clean and your heart is pure, let people say what they want and keep driving.

## Don't Fan the Flames

A local radio show host and good friend of mine, Austin Rhodes, the guy who actually helped me get my own show, was largely critical of me on certain issues while I was in office. He would try his best to goad me into responding. Unbeknownst to him, I had made it a point after taking office not to listen to his show, and I certainly was not going to take the bait from him when I knew the main thing he was looking for was ratings. Ultimately, the overwhelming support of the citizens I served was simply more important to me than the opinion of any one individual.

I'm of the mind-set that still waters run deep. When you're in the spotlight, you get people saying all kinds of negative things about you, especially with the convenience of social media. When you engage and respond, you just create a firestorm, and ultimately there's no winning that. Generally, when you let things go, there's no fuel to the fire and the flames eventually die out.

> When you engage and respond, you just create a firestorm, and ultimately there's no winning that. Generally, when you let things go, there's no fuel to the fire and the flames eventually die out.

While serving as mayor, I had a great relationship with our local media, and I'm glad to say I still do. But there was one instance where we had a controversy when Commissioner Marion Williams, a man of great passion, requested to see our city administrator Fred Russell's computer hard drive, believing Fred was conducting private business on his public computer. No one individual elected official can just request something like that, and in the end there didn't turn out to be anything on the hard drive even worthy of an investigation. But after the controversy had played itself out, I had a reporter with our local ABC affiliate want to stir things up again.

I always had an open-door policy with the press. When they would come into my office, I'd just say, "Well, what's the question?" In this instance, the reporter told me that he wanted to get my comment on the hard-drive issue that had long since passed. I said, "Look, all you're going to do is take my comment and show it to somebody else. And then you're going to get them to comment on my comment, and you're just going to breathe new life into a story that's old news."

I love the old saying: measure twice and cut once. As a Changemaker and as a leader, you need to know that your words have power. You don't need to let anybody rush you into making a statement that may be taken out of context or used to hurt someone.

## Patience Is a Virtue

It takes far more strength to hold your tongue in a disciplined manner than it does to release your tongue in anger. To reiterate my last point, words have consequences. So often we mistake the true meaning of strength—thinking of it as a show of force, or raising your voice, or acting stern. That is not necessarily strength. Undoubtedly, there is a time for those individual acts. But just because you're not losing your cool and not raising your voice does not at all mean that you're not strong. Sometimes silence is the best response.

Particularly, as a leader, if you're not well informed on a situation, and you don't know the complete story, I would use that strength *not* to comment. You're only feeding the situation if you're making comments based on half of the information on any given issue. It takes strength and discipline to take the time to get all the information that you need. Informed decisions are good decisions. It doesn't mean that you're dragging your feet if you're gathering the information to make a well-informed decision.

But in today's world, we're so impatient, we want everything *now*. It really takes strength to have the resolve and the courage not to be reactionary. As they say: patience is a virtue. And it is a critical skillset for a Changemaker.

I firmly believe that a love of learning teaches patience. Why? Because learning takes time. While in office, I needed to learn a lot of things, including getting to know the personalities of the people I worked with each and every day. That kind of relationship building takes time and patience. As I've mentioned previously, the political situation I was in, especially early on, was a bit contentious to say the least. But I was able to develop a strong working relationship with all our commissioners. Granted, they didn't always like my decisions, but they trusted and respected me.

> I firmly believe that a love of learning teaches patience. Why? Because learning takes time.

The structure of our local government is such that the mayor only votes in the event of a tie. The procedural maneuver of one of our ten commissioners abstaining from a vote to create a 5-4-1 outcome leading to no action taken by blocking the mayor's tie-breaking vote had become commonplace after our local government consolidated, and it had largely been a practice which had played out along racial lines. However, patiently developing trust with my colleagues led to me being afforded the opportunity to break more ties than I can begin to remember, which incidentally went very much under-reported. But the commissioners knew that I was going to be patient, calm, and consistent.

Any time I would break the tie, I would go with the recommendation of the administrator or the department head, because I had the mind-set of, "These people are trained and educated to do their job, so I'm not going to go with a political whim. I'm going to vote in favor of doing what the professionals recommend."

To give credit, I had developed this philosophy of taking a common sense approach to governing while serving on the board of the Family YMCA of Metro Augusta, many years earlier. We had brought on a new CEO named Danny McConnell, and he had asked for the board to consider expanding and redeveloping our flagship facility. The internal debate had become heated, and chief among the arguments against the expansion was the fact that soccer fields would be lost in the process. During the debate, Barry Storey, a good friend I've always admired for his wisdom and his statesmanlike approach to leadership, made a point that stuck with me from that moment forward when he said "Look, there's only one person in this room who has ever built a Y and that's Danny. We need to listen to him." The project was ultimately a success and I learned a great lesson that day and have often shared with Barry how I put his lesson to good use during my time in office.

## Leading Through a Time of Transition

When I was in office, Augusta was in a transitional period not unlike most mid-sized southern cities, a process which continues to this very day. I still remind people that we're no longer a small town with the city's population exceeding 200,000 residents, with 600,000 residents in our metropolitan statistical area. That being said, change is never easy and you're always going to experience growing pains, whether you're a business, a city, or any other organization.

In February of 2010, Augusta Pride announced that Augusta would be hosting our first Pride Parade. Most cities of our size in the south had already hosted these events, but this would be our first. As is so often the case, introducing any new event can create some difficulties, and there were those individuals and organizations who were dead set against Augusta hosting a Pride Parade ... period.

After the announcement was made, someone from within our local government leaked misinformation that the parade permit was sitting on my desk awaiting my signature and that the only thing standing between Augusta hosting or not hosting the event was me. I found it interesting that 2010 happened to be an election year, and I figured whoever "leaked" this bad information—the permit had in fact not yet made it through the process to my office for my signature—probably had political motivations for doing so. It was at that point when I began to receive angry calls, letters, and emails telling me that if I was to sign off on the parade, there would be political backlash and I would pay for it at the polls.

I once again figured that a calm, common sense approach would be the best course of action. I simply requested a legal opinion from our law department regarding the Augusta Pride organization having the legal right to have the parade, knowing what the answer would be based on freedom of speech. The affirmative legal opinion was turned around in a day, and at that point the permit was ready for me to sign, which I did. There was no holdup, and the first Augusta Pride event would go on that June as planned. However, political opponents and some media outlets did not see it that way, and I was pilloried for being indecisive and lacking backbone, as well as for dragging my feet for simply requesting a legal opinion. When he saw some of the negative press coverage which ensued, my good friend, US Army Brigadier General Jeff Foley, who was then serving as the commanding general at Fort Gordon, reached out to me to let me know that generals in the military always get a legal opinion before they make a decision. And fortunately, I had the support of leaders and friends throughout the community during the midst of the controversy.

During the time all this was going on, I had a meeting with the president of Augusta Pride, Isaac Kelly, and other organizers of the event at which they asked me to issue a proclamation declaring it Augusta Pride Day during the week of the event, which I agreed to do, and which ended up stirring up a bit more controversy. At the end of the meeting, I told the organizers "Look, I'll take the heat this year, and next year there won't be any controversy."

The inaugural event that year was ultimately embraced by the majority of our city and our community as a whole and was held with no incidences. Since then the event has grown every year, and in 2018 Augusta hosted our eighth annual Augusta Pride Week, which I believe reflects how far our city has transitioned into becoming a major part of the New South, while also retaining the best of our traditions, our values, and our character in the process.

# Handling the Recession by Watching Flight Attendants

We've all been there. The plane you're traveling on hits turbulence. Not just your regular type of turbulence, but the type that has glasses rattling, stomachs dropping, and the passengers around you closing their eyes in prayer. The first thing I always do in that situation is pretty simple: I look at the eyes of the flight attendants. If there's no fear there, then I figure everything will be okay. If I see fear, it's a totally different story.

When I first ran for mayor, I certainly didn't have any clue that I'd be in that type of leadership position in a city of 200,000 people when the worst recession in recent memory hit. As the nation faced an economic meltdown in September of 2008, I'd been in office for less than three years, and I remember wondering how this was going to impact the lives of the citizens I served, as well as the overall economy of our city. Things had been humming along at a rapid pace with big job announcements and our economic growth picking up pace. Would it just all grind to a halt? I didn't know the answer to that question, but I knew that whatever the case may be, I still had a city to lead.

Early on during the Great Recession, I made a choice based on my earlier observation of flight attendants during turbulence. Rather than showing fear and a lack of confidence to the public, I figured that if I stayed calm, stayed positive, and kept an upbeat attitude, it would help the people around me and the citizens I served to do the same thing. Each day I looked for something positive that I could share with our community during my many speaking engagements. I started writing a weekly highlights column that was distributed via email, social networking, and the city website. Day after day and week after week, I flooded the airwaves, internet, and the general public with positive news. It was never very hard to find; I just had to look for it and share it.

> Day after day and week after week, I flooded the airwaves, internet, and the general public with positive news. It was never very hard to find; I just had to look for it and share it.

The interesting and beautiful thing to me was to see the way people began to respond. Whether it was on my Facebook page, through emails and letters, or simply from a man or woman on the street, the positive energy I was putting out was coming back to me in spades. People constantly shared with me how blessed Augusta was to have been spared the brunt of the economic downturn and how excited they were about things going on in the city. Their kind words of affirmation had the effect of encouraging me daily and keeping me spiritually uplifted when times got tough. I will always consider myself fortunate to have experienced something so amazing when I continued to see story after story of the devastating toll the recession was having on cities around the country.

Being a Changemaker during the turbulent times of life can be a difficult situation to find yourself in. However, it's always good to remember that it is during these turbulent times that the people who depend on us need us the most. Staying calm, positive, and upbeat when life throws us the inevitable curveball can be a challenge, but based on my experience it's a challenge that's worth accepting. And the reward you'll receive in return for taking it far outweighs any difficulties you may encounter along the way.

# TWO CENTS FOR CHANGE

Fanning the flames of anger is simply not sustainable. It can rile people up for a short period of time, but as a Changemaker, to lead through anger is not sustainable, nor is it something that people will rally around for any length of time. Maintaining calmness and patience is absolutely critical. It's like the old adage about the slow drip, drip, drip of water—ultimately it wears away at the rocky ground and creates valleys for rivers to flow through. And remember, in the end most people are not naturally drawn to chaos, they're naturally drawn to calm.

1. Have you ever let your nerves keep you from making a decision during a time of adversity? In leadership positions, you're always going to have to face adversity and, although some might not want to admit it, testing your nerves can definitely come into play. Yet, I've always found that making decisions calms those nerves, whereas not making them generally only makes things worse.

2. Have you ever tried to be the calm at the center of the room in dealing with professional or personal adversity? During commission meetings, I sat in the middle of the dais, literally at the center of the body. By being at the focal point and through being the one to run the meetings, I always focused on being the calm at the center of the room. Although things could get contentious at times, it placed me in a position to set a tone for debate which usually contributed to issues we were dealing with being resolved as opposed to my using the position to fan the flames and keep the argument going.

3.  Do you take time to focus on maintaining a sense of calm for a few minutes each day? For me, this is taking time to pray and do my devotional in a quiet room each morning. I've always shared with people that taking that quiet time to start each day provides me a firm foundation to deal with whatever issues the day may bring.

4.  In your personal and professional life, do you gravitate toward calm or chaos? Let's face it, we all live chaotic lives these days to some degree or another. Personally, I've always gravitated toward calmness and trying to provide a sense of calm for others. I learned this from having mentors in my life to emulate, those who led in a calm, statesmanlike manner. Those mentors are still out there even in the midst of a chaotic world, and you just need to seek them out.

5.  Do you ever make the effort to truly unplug from the world around you? With modern technology, social networking, and the constant bombardment of words and images, it can seem like it's almost physically impossible to unplug from it all. But it can be done. I started a practice while in office that I continue to this day of putting my cell phone in the safe on vacations. While mayor, I told my executive assistants only to call me in the case of a crisis. In nine years, there were only two times they had to make that call, and the city never went to hell in a handbasket while my phone was in a safe.

chapter nine

# Character: Follow Your Moral Compass

*Fame is a vapor, popularity an accident, riches take wings. Only one thing endures and that is character.*

**—HORACE GREELY**

When I was a child and first moved to Augusta, my father did something that has stuck in my memory to this very day. My dad, Bill, had recently been named president and CEO of Columbia Nitrogen, a chemical company that primarily produced fertilizer. Growing up on a farm had instilled in him a lifelong love of the land,

and he absolutely loved to garden. Shortly after moving into our new home, he ordered a load of compost to start a vegetable garden. The garden was still there over forty years later when we sold the house after he passed, having produced a cornucopia of fresh vegetables for family, friends, and neighbors through the years.

When the first compost load was delivered, and the delivery truck was gone, I remember seeing a shiny, new wheelbarrow that had also been left behind. I remarked to my dad with childlike fascination how great I thought it was that someone had given him such a nice gift after we'd just moved to town. His reply to my observation? "I'm sending it back." At that point in life I couldn't fathom why anyone would want to send back a gift, particularly one that he could put to good use immediately. It just didn't make sense.

In his subtle way and as a man of few words, he took the time to sit me down and give me this explanation: "Once you start taking things from people you don't know, they're going to expect something from you and that's always gonna lead to a slippery slope." His simple, yet profound, words didn't fully register on me for many years, but they ended up having a deep impact on the way I conducted my business when I was elected to the mayor's office decades later.

> Once you start taking things from people you don't know, they're going to expect something from you and that's always gonna lead to a slippery slope.

Coming in to office, my eyes were wide open as to what a large percentage of people thought politicians use their office for personal gain. I'd say that this is painting with a broad brush, as there are many good people who offer themselves for service in elected office and have very distinguished careers in public service. However, with the knowledge of what many citizens thought, I determined I'd do things a bit differently.

During my time in office, I did something pretty simple: I took my dad's advice. I knew going in there was a line where things would become a slippery slope in a hurry, and I just decided to stay as far away from it as I possibly could. Fortunately, I was very blessed to have outside resources that put me in a position to choose this path, something I never took for granted, as it allowed me to do things like pay for my own gas, meals, and most of my travel expenses. With the wheelbarrow analogy in mind, I simply tried to steer clear of people I didn't know giving me things—as my dad had laid out all those years before just where that could lead.

My time in office wasn't perfect by any means, and I know that, like everyone else who has ever served, I made some mistakes along the way. I can speak firsthand to the fact that keeping your ego in check in leadership positions can be hard work at times, and surrounding yourself with people who keep you grounded is an absolute must. That being said, I firmly believe that the principle not accepting the shiny, new wheelbarrows along the way both made a difference and made things easier

> Keeping your ego in check in leadership positions can be hard work at times, and surrounding yourself with people who keep you grounded is an absolute must.

for me, and I'll always be grateful to my dad for sharing that little pearl of wisdom with me at a very young age.

When it comes to character and the art of becoming a better leader, my father has always been my true north.

## The Most Precious Garden

My father grew up on a farm in a small town, Tazewell, Virginia, and his father passed from pneumonia when Dad was only twelve. So, they ended up moving to Blacksburg, where my grandmother, Fern, was a school teacher who raised five kids during the Great Depression. But his love of farming and gardening always went with him. He loved growing absolutely beautiful roses, and he instilled in me a love for planting seeds, nurturing things, and watching them grow. My mother loved gardening as well, so I came by it naturally and know that despite their political differences, this love of the land was something that always bound my parents together.

Dad had the most wonderful vegetable garden as well and was proud to share the vegetables he had grown with his family and friends. Nurturing those seeds to fruition and being able to share the crop of fruits and vegetables with others was truly my father's focus. As Changemakers, we should be focused on nurturing seeds, then sharing the bounty by taking care of our neighbors and the people around us.

Our priority should be to nurture and care for the areas of the greatest need first. That's why my focus while in office was in redeveloping and revitalizing the Laney Walker/Bethlehem neighborhood. I saw that as being one of the lowest-income areas of the city and, therefore, had the most need. To plant the seeds within that area of the city that have now grown to fruition, and continues to grow, was extremely important to me because that was where the greatest need was. I'm proud to say that these efforts to revitalize a long disinvested neighborhood did not go unnoticed at the state and national levels, winning multiple awards including the Georgia Planning Association's Outstanding Implementation Award The efforts were also recognized by Harvard University's School of Design's Student Journal on Real Estate as potentially being a "game-changing" national model for public/private partnerships.[3]

Nurturing seeds takes time, and it takes a love for what you're nurturing. I took that with me into office, realizing that out of the seeds I helped to plant, a lot of them weren't going to come to fruition until after I was long gone. But I was willing to help plant them and nurture them during my time, and hopefully I'm continuing to do that not just in Augusta, but in other places now that I'm out of office.

## The Only Thing That Endures

When I first took office, we were facing a deficit, so we asked the department heads to cut a certain percentage out of their own budget. My budget was primarily salaries, but the membership to the US Conference of Mayors cost $10,000 per year. I will say the US Conference of Mayors is a great organization that does a tremendous amount of good, but I just couldn't ask the department heads to cut their budgets if I was unwilling to cut mine. My character wouldn't allow it. Therefore, I cut the membership.

When I first took office, and throughout my time there, people would ask me, "Why don't you just publicly call out your colleagues on issues?" I shared with them: "that's not my character nor who I am." The values instilled in me were to treat everybody with professionalism, dignity, and respect. I wasn't about to compromise my character for what was politically expedient. Too often we see elected officials and politicians compromising their character, doing things that are out of character to win an election. A Changemaker would

---

3    Neil Gordon, "Laney Walker Development Getting Some Attention," Buzz on Biz, June 21, 2012, http://buzzon.biz/2012/06/laney-walker-development-getting-some-attention/.

rather lose than compromise his or her character. To compromise your character to achieve any goal says to me that the goal really isn't worth achieving.

There's a new strategy, it seems, where you do whatever you have to do, say whatever you have to say, and act however you have to act to win an election, even if it's out of character. Politics as usual says that you have to conform to a certain ideal of what a politician should be. Yet somehow maintaining my integrity and character helped me win three elections even if it flew in the face of conventional political wisdom.

Changemakers need to trust their instincts, their moral compass. If you do something that you know is going against what your moral compass and your instincts tell you to do, it's ultimately compromising your integrity. And while compromising your integrity may get you the desired outcome in the short run, it will always lead to a loss in the long run. It goes back to the slippery slope of the wheelbarrow. Once you compromise your integrity on one decision, then the slippery slope kicks in. You ultimately box yourself in. And before long comes the snowball effect.

> While compromising your integrity may get you the desired outcome in the short run, it will always lead to a loss in the long run.

You have to realize that actions have consequences, and nothing happens in a vacuum. You need to take a deep breath and think about the consequences of your actions. The ripple effect works both ways, bad and good. The decisions you make in a leadership position or as a Changemaker have a ripple and long-lasting impact. I've witnessed that firsthand; when people in leadership positions make decisions in vacuums, you can safely bet that the law of unintended consequences will kick in shortly thereafter. It's better to take a moment, take a deep breath, and make the *right* decision than to make the wrong decision in haste.

There's a great song by Australian folksinger, Paul Kelly, who I was introduced to by my friend, Gavin Hobson, during my time in Australia in my twenties: "From Little Things, Big Things Grow." To avoid a snowball effect or a chain reaction, check yourself on that first decision you have to make that calls your integrity into question. Maintain your integrity at all costs, because if you want to be a Changemaker in your business, in your district, or in your community, you have to have credibility.

And once you lose your credibility, your ability to be a Changemaker goes with it.

> And once you lose your credibility, your ability to be a Changemaker goes with it.

## Running the Land Trust

When I was a partner in the Sotheby's office in Beaufort, South Carolina, I established the principle that I would never sell anybody a piece of property I wouldn't buy myself. It was the same thing during my time serving as executive director of the Central Savannah River Land Trust: I would never ask anybody to give to a cause that I wouldn't give to myself. Part of my job was running the Greenspace Program for the city of Augusta, which was a land-buying program to buy up open space. There was a piece of property that was in a floodplain, so basically it couldn't be developed. The commissioner who then represented the district called me and said, "We need to buy this piece of property. This property owner is down my throat on this," basically just wanting to get the guy out of his hair.

In real estate, price per acre matters. If we overpaid, that would impact every one of our future purchases, and the city would have to overpay for floodplain property going forward. "I'm just not willing to make that recommendation," I told him. "That kind of knee-jerk reaction to get a citizen out of your hair by overpaying for a piece of property will cost the city much more money in the long run."

Even though the commissioner wanted me to make a decision that was politically expedient, I just wasn't willing to compromise my integrity to do it. In the long run, we got the property below the asking price. And today it's a beautiful piece of greenspace, just a stone's throw away from the home where we now live.

## Use the Good China

I have a very strong relationship with our military. I think part of that comes from my father going into the US Army Air Corps at the age of seventeen. He effectively learned a lot about what it was to be a man of integrity through his military service. Those values he passed on to me, those four pillars of character: duty, honor, integrity, and service above self. Yet I would say from my own experiences and lessons in leadership and changemaking, that *compassion* is the *fifth* pillar of character.

You have to have compassion for the people around you. Unless you value others, how can you be putting service to them above your own self-interest?

When I was seventeen, I worked laying tile for a group called Mastercraft Flooring. Actually, I was one of their first employees. And it was then that I used to go into the Laney Walker/Bethlehem neighborhood. They had me go pick up the craftsmen, generally older African-American gentlemen who didn't have driver's licenses. I had spent time in those neighborhoods, I'd seen the needs of the people. So, years later after I was elected mayor, I knew what needed to be done. Having had that cultural experience gave me not just compassion for the neighborhood, but empathy about the conditions that people are in, and a passion about doing something about it.

Not long ago, Malisa and I had a kickoff party at our house for a large community project I was involved in. Two friends of mine, African-American commissioners of Augusta, were sitting there eating, so I wandered over and sat down with them. They said, "You know, Mr. Mayor, we go to these events all the time, and we're eating off of plastic plates. But we can't believe that your wife's serving us off of your china." It hit me at that point the things we take for granted. They were guests in my house, and Malisa and I were taught that guests always get the fine china.

People appreciate being included, and true character means you have to reach out to *everybody*. You have to be willing to set aside your own self-interest, your own preconceived notions, and your own biases to open yourself up. That is character, and that's what builds bonds of respect and trust. That's how you make positive impact and become a better leader.

Changemakers must be willing to serve *everybody* on their fine china.

> Changemakers must be willing to serve *everybody* on their fine china.

## The Right Thing

In today's world it seems as though there's no shortage of examples of leaders being compromised by ethical issues. Whether it's corporate CEOs, elected officials, non-profit executives, or the heads of organizations at all levels, the headlines are full of examples of what not to do in a leadership position—and the same type scenario seems to repeat itself with an unnerving frequency.

I remember asking my father—who, again, was a very ethical CEO, loved by his employees and respected by his peers—some ideas for topics for a public-speaking class I was taking back in college. His number-one response came as a surprise to me, although in retrospect it probably shouldn't have: business ethics. He went on to explain to me his view that issues with business ethics would become an epidemic in the future … and, unfortunately, he was right on target.

Looking back, I think my wise father was using this topic as a teaching experience for me more than a way to help hone my public-speaking skills. As this was during the early nineties, my research and subsequent speech predated many of the major political and corporate scandals which have transpired since. However, more importantly for me personally is the fact that my father's turning my attention toward this issue predated my chairing boards of directors, helping to run a small business, running a non-profit, and ultimately serving as mayor of Augusta, Georgia.

Through the years I've become fascinated by the transformative power of truly ethical leadership and the lasting impact Changemakers who lead from the heart can have on the organizations they serve. In discussions on this topic, it always seems that the common denominator of what the average men or women on the street want to see from their leaders is relatively simple: they want leaders who are transparent, they want leaders who serve the greater good, and they want leaders who simply "do the right thing." The first two principles are more or less easy to grasp and understand, and we have many examples of leaders who are transparent and who've focused on serving the greater good. However, for a leader to "do the right thing" in the eyes of those they serve gets to be a bit trickier and entails truly learning to trust your instincts while at the same time leading from your heart.

Having experienced the world of politics firsthand, I've come to understand that the idea of "doing the right thing" is subjective, and, ultimately, the right thing for one constituency might not be the right thing for another. However, I also found that doing the right thing ties directly back into and was a fundamental part of another of the inherent things people expect of their leaders: serving the greater good. During my early experiences in leadership positions, I was able to develop my instincts with regard to making decisions based on the greater good of any organization I served while not catering to any one given constituency. In retrospect, this experience was invaluable when I decided to become a public servant.

It always seems that the common denominator of what the average men or women on the street want to see from their leaders is relatively simple: they want leaders who are transparent, they want leaders who serve the greater good, and they want leaders who simply "do the right thing."

After being elected in 2005, I was well aware I had never served an organization comprised of 2,700 employees and 200,000 citizens (whom I viewed to a large degree as valued shareholders in the city), and that any decision I made was going to make someone mad.

However, I realized early on that no matter the size of the organization, this simple principle holds true: if you're fair in your decision-making and you can easily explain your reasons for making the decisions you've made, you quickly develop an invaluable reserve of trust and respect within the people whom your decisions impact as a whole. With this principle firmly at the core of my decision-making process I was able to build public trust in my leadership while serving for nine years in office and being elected three times with an average of 64 percent of the vote.

> If you're fair in your decision-making and you can easily explain your reasons for making the decisions you've made, you quickly develop an invaluable reserve of trust and respect within the people whom your decisions impact as a whole.

Leading from the heart, trusting my instincts, and focusing on serving the greater good were put to a major test during my final year in office. For seven years prior, the city had implemented no tax increases, while at the same time going several years without giving our employees raises, thus putting our city finances between a rock and a hard place. Prior to public meetings on the potential tax increase, eight of my elected colleagues on our ten-member board of commissioners had voted in favor of the increase. However, after a limited, but very vocal, number of people in attendance at the public meetings voiced their great displeasure with the proposal, the original eight votes were no longer there.

When the proposal finally came before the body, the votes *for* and *against* fell into a five/five tie, with my vote serving as the tie-breaker. Without hesitation, I voted in favor of the tax increase, both allowing for employees to get raises and to increase much needed revenue flow into our city's operational budget. The reasoning for my decision was simply based on sound business principles. In order for a business to be sustainably successful, and to maintain staff morale, employees must be valued and rewarded over time for their hard work. At the same time, no business can operate functionally over time without increased revenues, because expenses (gas, electricity, etc.) continue to increase for a city just like any other business. Though I certainly didn't want to raise taxes, in this case serving the greater good meant having to make a decision I knew wouldn't sit well with some people.

Although many of my colleagues thought my decision would lead to a public outcry against me, in the end that was not at all the case. Ultimately, I received three angry emails and one public rebuke. It's interesting to note that I also received very vocal public support from the citizen on the street applauding my decision as people understood my reasoning for it. I even got a high five out of it while I was out on an afternoon run. My instincts had been correct, and the vocal minority against the tax increase had been just that: a vocal *minority*. My decision had both served the greater good and been the right thing to do.

Learning to trust your instincts, to serve the greater good, and to lead from the heart is not an easy proposition. Many times, it will place you in positions where your leadership may be questioned, and your decisions may very well seem counterintuitive to public opinion or the sentiment of vocal constituencies within whatever organization your leadership role may serve.

However, at the end of the day, a focus on decisions made through time-tested good instincts and on behalf of the greater good will undoubtedly lead to you becoming a more trusted and respected leader and a Changemaker. It will also lead to your leadership role having a lasting impact, which will serve your organization long after your season of leadership is over.

*The Metro Spirit* is our weekly paper, and that publication wasn't always a fan of mine. During my first year in office, their "Insider" column (with no byline) repeatedly took aim at me with critical remarks that I, and many others, felt were only opinions and not necessarily based in fact. It ultimately got so bad that the Family YMCA of Metro Augusta, an organization whose board I had once chaired and one of the publication's major distribution points, had the *Spirit's* racks pulled from all their locations. Shortly thereafter, I received a call from their editor, Joe White, a man I'd never met. He shared with me the financial impact this would have on the publication. Although I didn't like what they had to say about me, I had grown up a fan of good journalism and a supporter of freedom of speech. After we spoke, I called the CEO of the Family YMCA and requested that he put the racks back in the facilities, which he agreed to do.

In the fall of 2018, I received a call from Joe, with whom I'd developed a friendship with over the years, letting me know that his readers had voted me "Best Politician" four years after leaving office. Although I'm no longer a politician, this unexpected news underscored for me that leading through character and integrity always has a lasting impact.

Doing it the right way—the way my father taught me—and having the citizens of this community still consider me to be a change-making leader four years removed from office is truly humbling, and something I will always appreciate.

**TWO CENTS FOR CHANGE**

In the end, enduring character is ultimately what matters most in order to be a Changemaker. Character is like a muscle that grows stronger the more it's developed through life's trials and tribulations as well as through both victory and defeat along the way. Exercising it can be difficult at times, as it often leads to taking the road less traveled and going against the grain, but maintaining your integrity and keeping a good name for yourself in a leadership position is the only way you're ever going to help create enduring positive change. And remember, always keeping to the high ground has an added benefit to your changemaking endeavors: it makes you much harder to hit when people inevitably start taking shots at you!

1. Have you ever compromised your character in an effort to further yourself in your personal or professional life? None of us are perfect, and we live in a society where winning can be portrayed to be everything. However, compromising your character is one of the most direct routes to the slippery slope I touched on earlier, and a slope usually leads to an edge you'll want to steer clear of.

2. Have you ever sought out mentors and role models who demonstrate what good character looks like? As I mentioned earlier, my dad was and is my true north in matters of character. But there are many other individuals in every sector who lead through enduring character. It may not be as much the norm these days, but I would highly recommend seeking them out and making this a primary focus in your leadership endeavors.

3.  What is the character trait you most highly admire and
    try to integrate into your professional and personal life?
    The character traits I learned through my father were based
    largely on his military service, but it doesn't need to be
    the same for everybody. Things like loyalty, honesty, and
    forgiveness are also extraordinarily important in leadership
    positions, and I'm sure you can all build on this list.

4.  What is a character trait which causes you to pause and
    to doubt following a leader who exhibits it? Machiavellian
    leadership can lead to success in both business and politics
    but leading through fear and intimidation rarely leads to
    people willingly following a leader. Think about how a dic-
    tatorial leadership style can inhibit your willingness to be
    a part of the process.

5.  What does enduring character mean to you? In the end,
    character can be subjective at times but however you define
    it, it simply matters. Identifying what it means to you
    and the team around you is a key attribute to becoming a
    Changemaker and should always define the mission of any
    organization you serve.

a
parting
word

# Passing the Baton to the Next Changemakers

*One of the most vital roles of a Changemaker is to look beyond his or her time in any given leadership position with a strong commitment toward cultivating and supporting a new generation of leaders.*

## —DEKE COPENHAVER

It's certainly not news to anyone reading this that we live in a fast-changing world, with the pace of change growing exponentially every day. When we scan the horizon, we'll see no small number of anxiety-ridden individuals and organizations seeking to stop change or go back to what they perceive to be a simpler time, by clinging to the status quo as a safety net. A "but we've always done it this way" mind-set is futile in a world where the reality is if we don't embrace and adjust to change, as scary as it may be, we get run over by it. The businesses where we work and the communities in which we live are either moving forward or moving backwards, as the world around us simply doesn't sit still.

> **If we don't embrace and adjust to change, as scary as it may be, we get run over by it.**

For leaders, part of adjusting to change means coming to grips with the reality that we must pass the baton of leadership willingly as opposed to holding onto it with a clinched fist. In order for our cities and our businesses to be sustainable, new leadership over time isn't just a nicety, it's a necessity. Having the ability to recruit and retain the best and brightest young minds possible is ultimately the lifeblood of any organization. To keep this lifeblood flowing, the next generation of leaders must not simply be analyzed and categorized, they must be engaged.

> **New leadership over time isn't just a nicety, it's a necessity.**

I've often found myself in board meetings or on task forces where one particular question seems to come up again and again: how do we engage millennials? Ironically, nine times out of ten there's no one under the age of forty sitting in the room. In speaking to my younger friends about this situation, there seems to be a consensus that their voices aren't being heard because they're generally not included in these discussions, and if they are, they're talked over and not with.

Growing up and during my young adult life, I was blessed to have many mentors, with my father chief among them. I remember being taught life lessons by men and women who shared them willingly, which has benefited me in every role I've occupied as an adult. Through this experience I learned the power of mentoring which has given me a great passion for engaging the younger generation of Augusta's citizens. Exchanging ideas and points of view with a group of millennial entrepreneurs, artists, and business owners on a regular basis keeps me energized about the future of our city and inspires me to continue to work toward fulfilling its vast potential. For my younger friends, I provide a sounding board and am able to share some of my own lessons learned through my time in business as well as in the public sector. At the end of the day, it's simply a win/win situation.

Change can be a scary thing, and realizing that it's time to pass the baton of leadership to the generation behind us is not an easy idea to confront. However, taking the time to engage, mentor, and teach a new generation of leaders can be an extraordinarily inspiring experience, benefiting all generations involved in the process. Learning across generations is simply one of the coolest things I've ever experienced, and I've found that *every* generation has something to teach us.

I've always viewed my life as playing itself out in chapters, and as I enter into a new chapter of my life, I'm extremely glad to have you all along for the ride. I hope that in some way this book has helped you in your life—because the desire to help people has always been at the core of any endeavor I've ever undertaken. Please know how much I appreciate you all taking the time to read this book, because time is a valuable commodity that none of us can ever get enough of.

So, what comes next you may ask? For me, it's using this book as a platform to inspire Changemakers everywhere to take a leap of faith and join together in making a positive impact on their businesses, their communities, and in their personal lives. For you, I'm hopeful you will take some of the life lessons I've shared and use them to help give you the hope and courage to take that leap of faith to become a Changemaker.

My life has taken a circuitous path along the way that has allowed me to intersect with amazing and inspirational people from all walks of life during its many twists and turns. I've pursued an unconventional road, with forays into the worlds of business, nonprofit work, elected office, and the media. I know what it's like to build a small business and serve nonprofits from a volunteer and professional perspective, while at the same time serving on the boards of foundations which help provide funding to organizations which need it most. I've seen firsthand what it's like to be on both sides of the microphone—being interviewed for nine years in office and doing interviews for nearly a year as part of our local media in a successful radio show that defied convention. Each experience has blessed me with a unique and balanced perspective on the issues facing our businesses, our communities, and our nation from

> My personal mission with every platform I've been given has been to simply build stronger communities, stronger organizations, and stronger individuals.

real-world experience, which I hope will ultimately have a lasting positive impact through sharing what I've learned with others. Ultimately, my personal mission with every platform I've been given has been to simply build stronger communities, stronger organizations, and stronger individuals, and I'm extremely encouraged that the platform provided me by the Advantage|ForbesBooks team will provide an avenue to move my life's mission beyond our local community ... and to share it with *you.*

Today, I'm at the helm of a growing niche consulting firm, with a wide array of clients from the business, nonprofit, and economic-development worlds, whose efforts I'm dedicated to supplementing in an effort to further my mission and the mission of my business to build stronger communities at every level. And in the end, it's my great hope that through this book we can work together to make our world a better place one community at a time, and that one day our paths will cross somewhere out there on the road less traveled!

# more from deke

## Speaking:

Are you looking for a dynamic speaker who will change the lives of your audience forever? Well, look no further. Deke has been inspiring crowds for over a decade at speaking engagements for organizations like the International Association of Outsourcing Professionals World Summit, TedX Augusta, the Robin Hood Foundation Veterans Summit, the Philips Healthcare Mega Meeting, the Bermuda Community Foundation, and METal International. To book Deke as a speaker go to www.dekecopenhaver.com.

## Consulting:

Is your business or organization in need of a change? How about a Changemaker? Copenhaver Consulting serves businesses and individuals across a variety of sectors including nonprofits, small businesses, economic-development organizations, and local governments. For a free consultation email us at info@copenhaverconsulting.com.

## Media relations:

Maintaining a good working relationship with the media is a must for individuals in leadership positions and organizations alike. Copenhaver Consulting uses Deke's real-world experience in cultivating positive media relations derived from nine years in office and hosting a daily radio show to help individuals and organizations alike build better media relations. For more information email us at info@copenhaverconsulting.com.

## Public relations:

Positive public relations for your business and your personal brand are a must in today's world. Copenhaver Consulting can help develop proactive strategies for maintaining a positive public presence for both. For more information email us at info@copenhaverconsulting.com.

## Blog:

Check out Deke's monthly blog at www.dekecopenhaver.com

## Writing:

Check out Deke's monthly column on leadership published by the Georgia Municipal Association at www.gmanet.com

My first campaign in 2005.

Top: My first day in office at our first Prayer Breakfast.
Bottom: With Chick-fil-A founder, Truett Cathey.

My first year in office in 2006.

Throwing out the first pitch at an Augusta Greenjackets game.

Visiting my father during my second campaign in 2006.

Top: Celebrating the Augusta Greenjackets Southeast Atlantic League title with Cal Ripken Jr.
Bottom: At the groundbreaking of the $170 million Starbucks facility in Augusta.

Competing in the IRONMAN August 70.3.

With Malisa in my third and final campaign in 2010.

Speaking at the Robin Hood Foundation's Veteran's Summit on the *USS Intrepid* in New York.

Top: Riding in the Martin Luther King Jr. Day parade in Augusta.
Bottom: Declaring it Lady Antebellum Day in Augusta.

Speaking at a change of command ceremony at Fort Gordon.

Top: With Governor Nathan Deal and Columbia County Commission Chairman Ron Cross during the ice storm in 2014.
Bottom: Speaking at the Authority Insiders Forum in Atlanta.

With Malisa at the premiere of the James Brown biopic *Get on Up* in 2014.

My final year in office in 2014 with our corgi, Sarah Bet.